ABBA'S

Wholeness Through Intimacy

Owen Lovejoy

Owen Lovejoy
Abba's Heart Mission International
220 Pine Grove Rd.
Black Mountain, NC 28711
Email: olovejoy@hotmail.com

All Scripture quotations taken from the NEW AMERICAN STANDARD BIBLE, © 1960, 1962, 1963, 1968, 1971, 1972, 1973, 1975, 1977, 1995 by The Lockman Foundation. Used by permission. www.Lockman.org

The Hands sketch on the title page was drawn by Lutz Scherneck.

The Eagle sketch on the last page was drawn by Ken Modak.

ISBN 978-1495912627

CONTENTS

ACKNOWLEDGMENTS

I am grateful to these friends who have read my manuscript and offered valuable commentary: Amy Donaldson, Miriam Hayes, Bonnie Kaminski and Stephanie Gibson.

Others have known about this book project from the beginning and have continually encouraged me towards its completion. Although there have been many encouragers along the way, Kerah Fredrikson, Dotti Simmons and Betty Jo Gill especially invested themselves by praying for me and this book.

Other friends have played a crucial role in my journey to wholeness. I cannot adequately express my thanks to Melba Banks and John and Debra Rice.

At the outset of our dark season, our grandchildren, unbeknownst to them, infused our lives with joy. They continue to open our hearts to love in new and dynamic ways!

For my talented friends, Lutz Scherneck and Ken Modak, thank you for the beautiful sketches of the hands and the eagle.

Lastly, my greatest supporter and daily encourager is my wife, Anita. I am so blessed!

For Mom and Erin

PREFACE

There are many legitimate names for God found in the Bible. Throughout this book, I most often use the name *Abba* when referring to God. Although further explanation of that name comes later, I want to say up front that *Abba* is an Aramaic term of endearment used to address one's father. *Abba* is used several times in the New Testament in reference to God. In these pages I want to emphasize the intimate relationship God desires with us, therefore I use the name *Abba* to reflect the longing of His heart. As you read, substitute whatever term best expresses your longing of intimacy with the heavenly Father.

Prologue

After thirteen years of pastoring the same church, I needed a change. I love teaching, especially the Bible. When an opportunity opened to teach at a small Bible College in the Midwest, I was ecstatic. The pay was not great and the school could not afford to help us move, but my wife and I still felt a sense of excitement in this new adventure.

I knew only a few people at the Bible College, the President and two teachers. The President was a soft-spoken, well-educated man. I greatly respected him. I had never met the Vice President of Academic Affairs. He was the son of the school's founder.

The school year started smoothly enough. I immersed myself in preparation and in teaching. Most of the students were hungry for God and a delight to teach. As the first quarter progressed, however, disturbing patterns surfaced.

One disturbing pattern was the autocratic nature of the school's leadership. Although the teachers at this school were referred to as *elders*, we were clearly informed that the title of *elder* did not carry with it any authority. All decisions were made by the President and the Vice President of Academic Affairs. Although the teachers were encouraged to express their concerns at the leadership meetings, retribution was unleashed against any who questioned decisions or challenged the status quo. I learned that too late.

In a leadership meeting I gave voice to a very real problem in the student body. A 35 year old divorced male student was harassing female students and making suggestive and inappropriate remarks to some minor children of adult students. He had already precipitated the departure of at least one young female student from the school and was making life unbearable for other females. In addition, he was sowing seeds of discord and dissension among the young males of the school. Even residents of the local town made complaints about the student. All of those details were known by the Vice President and at least some details were known by the President. At a faculty meeting, I questioned why the offending predatory student was permitted to remain.

One week after expressing my opinions, another faculty meeting was called. When I arrived at that meeting, only one chair, in a prominent position, remained empty. Unbeknownst to me, I was the sole topic on the agenda of the meeting. First the Vice President then the President made false accusations against me. As they reviewed the history of the situation, they twisted some details and omitted others, all for the purpose of vilifying me. The President taunted me with my own words, taken out of context, which I had shared with him in confidence. In retrospect I saw that not only was their pride wounded, but they wanted to deflect attention from the predatory student. They also needed a new villain in order to cover up their gross negligence. I was the most obvious choice. Although every accusation left a deep wound, the last thrust was the deadliest. The President condemned me with words that I had never heard spoken to an unbeliever, let alone a believer. I felt like I was in a nightmare. The days and weeks following that meeting were marked by the rapid decline of my health: spiritual, emotional and physical.

I admit that the problems I refer to at the school reflect my own perceptions. Not everyone would agree with me, but many would. One thing is indisputable: I was devastated and nearly destroyed by those who were in authority at the Bible College. I don't think they intended to destroy me, just discredit me, but that is no excuse for their abuse of power. May God forgive them.

Note: Although a prologue comes before the main body of a literary work, it is the last thing written in this book. I wrote each chapter as God completed different phases of my healing. I added this prologue to give the reader better insight into the source of my devastation.

If most chapters seem to be penned by an author in the midst of a crisis, I can assure you that was the case. But I hope you will keep reading to the end and find hope in the God who loves you.

Blessings to you as you read!

Owen Lovejoy
Abba's Heart Mission International
Black Mountain, North Carolina

INTRODUCTION

Katrina

In August, 2005 a hurricane devastated New Orleans and much of the Gulf Coast. The hurricane itself only lasted a few hours; the aftermath however, has lasted many months. They called the hurricane, *Katrina.*

I use *Katrina* as a metaphor for my own personal storm. Similarly, the initial blow of my Katrina, though devastating, only lasted a short time, but the aftermath has lasted months. My storm came in the form of words. How can simple words be considered a storm? Although my storm is not comparable to the suffering caused by the hurricane, yet Proverbs tells us that "life and death are in the power of the tongue." When the verbal blow hit, I felt as though a six inch knife had been thrust into my gut. I found breathing difficult. Shock and disbelief overwhelmed me like waves. I cried out to Jesus, "Where are You?"; "Why is this happening to me?" I heard no explanation. This verbal assault did not come from an unbeliever or an immature Christian. To the contrary, it came from a sincere, mature, trusted Christian in a position of authority. That made the blow all the more grievous and damaging. As with the hurricane, I am still recovering many months later. Without a doubt, a physical knife wound in the gut would have healed far quicker than this wound inflicted with words. The original emotional wound festered and manifested itself in physical symptoms also.

I write this account, not to dwell on the wound or the circumstances in which it was given. I intend to focus on the God of all mercy who loves us and desires to bring us up out of the pit, out of the miry clay, to set our feet upon the rock and put a new song in our mouths, a song of praise to our God (Psalm 40:2,3). I pray that my story will be a source of encouragement to all those who currently find themselves in a pit, regardless of the depth or dimension, and who realize they cannot extricate themselves. I encourage you to cry out to the Lord and wait patiently for Him (Psalm 40:1).

Prayer: Dear Abba, you hear the cry of the bruised and the brokenhearted. A bruised reed you will not crush! You are the God of all comfort. You draw close to the hurting. Come to the needy who read these pages. Bring a healing balm in your hand. Reveal Your overwhelming and unfathomable love for them- *personally*; the love of a perfect Father for His children; the love of Abba's heart.

Chapter 1: Let It Go!

"Not forsaking our own assembling together, as is the habit of some, but encouraging one another..." Hebrews 10:25

"With all prayer and petition praying at all times in the Spirit. . .for all the saints." Ephesians 6:18

"Be kind to one another, tender-hearted, forgiving each other, just as God in Christ also has forgiven you." Ephesians 4:32

I so appreciate the people of God! If you are not involved in a local church of praying and believing Christians, I hope you will soon find one. Abba's children have prayed for me, encouraged me, and given me messages from Him. They have been instrumental in my climb out of the pit.

Abba used Bob to help me take my first step upward. Sitting in church one Sunday morning, God spoke these words to Bob's heart: "Let it go!" Bob could not figure out what the words meant, or how they applied to him. He happened to glance my direction and when his gaze fell upon me, the words came again, "*He* needs to let it go." Bob called me that afternoon and asked if he could visit me. He and others knew I was not well, but he did not know any details of my struggle. Although I normally had a joyful nature, I seldom laughed anymore. I had lost weight at an alarming rate. My countenance mirrored my soul's condition—not good! Our children asked my wife what had happened to me. They noted my downward spiral. Bob did not know that I could not sleep at night or that my digestion felt like a chemistry experiment gone bad. He did not know that I was at the bottom of a pit. He came and shared the words God spoke to him, but which he could not interpret. I knew exactly what they meant.

"Let it go!" For months I had been agonizing over my Katrina encounter, replaying the scene in my mind again and again.

"How should I have responded?" "What should I have said or not said?" "Why didn't someone help me?" "Why didn't God help me?" When I heard the words, "Let it go!" I clearly understood that I needed to move on. I needed to get out of my recliner, out of the house, out of my self-preoccupation and move forward. Within a few days, God instructed me to complete several specific actions in keeping with His word to let go. With His help, I complied. "Let it go" meant more than overt actions; it meant I needed to forgive also. The need to forgive started with those involved in my "Katrina," but it didn't stop there. The need to forgive mushroomed into a major heart-searching, heart-cleansing, and life-giving work of Abba in my life. Praise Him!

I knew the theological reasons for forgiving. The Lord's Prayer clearly states that in order to be forgiven by God, we must forgive our debtors. Forgiveness or the lack thereof carries eternal consequences. But forgiving someone from the heart requires more than acknowledging a scriptural principle. The well-known parable in Matthew 18 begins with Peter asking Jesus, "Lord, how often shall my brother sin against me and I forgive him? Up to seven times?" (the number of completion, the fulfillment of all duty). Jesus responds: "I do not say to you, up to seven times, but up to seventy times seven." (No matter how many times your brother sins against you, don't even think about withholding forgiveness!) Then Jesus responds to Peter's question with a parable. A summary goes like this:

> A king wanted to settle accounts with his slaves. In the process, there came into his presence a slave that owed him ten thousand talents. Without going into higher math, we can safely assume this debt could **never** be paid by the slave (The debt would translate into many millions of dollars today). The king planned to liquidate all that the slave possessed. When the slave begged for mercy, the king felt compassion for him and forgave him his entire debt.

The forgiven slave then went out looking for a fellow slave who owed him a much smaller amount, a sum that actually **could** be paid back over a reasonable amount of time. The second slave begged for patience and mercy just as the forgiven slave had done, but he received none. The forgiven slave had his fellow slave thrown into prison because he could not immediately repay the debt. The end of the story is not pleasant for the original, forgiven slave. When the king discovered the callous lack of charity and compassion on the part of the slave who had received great charity and compassion, he became angry, reinstated the slave's debt, and had him bound and thrown into prison.

At first glance, this parable merely reinforces the same idea as the Lord's Prayer: "If you want to be forgiven, you'd better forgive!" But there is more to it than that. One clue comes from the size of the first slave's debt. No slave could have amassed a ten-thousand-talent debt. There must be a point in Jesus using such an incredible sum. Jesus' implied message looks like this:

> *If Abba has forgiven you, Peter,* (you may want to replace Peter's name with your own) *a debt which you could never repay in one hundred lifetimes, then naturally* (due to Abba's supernatural working in your heart) *you will gladly forgive your brother's debt which is minuscule in comparison.*

The parable also offers us a motivation for forgiving, other than fear. Abba's heart of compassion alone can move us to forgive from our hearts. Generally, a parable has one central theme or message. The central theme of this parable reveals Abba's heart of compassion as the primary motivation for us to forgive.

Phil helped me see that truth clearly. I was leading a Bible study using this parable in Matthew 18. After discussing the parable I asked for volunteers to act it out. Dave, a retired Navy chief with a big voice, volunteered to be the king. Olivia, a college student, volunteered to be the second servant. Then Phil, a gentle and kind-hearted man with autism, volunteered to be the first servant. Phil had an uncanny ability with numbers, but more importantly, he was the most child-like adult I have ever met.

King Dave proceeded to call Servant Phil to settle accounts. Phil confessed that he did not have the funds to repay King Dave but pleading for the king's patience and mercy, he promised to pay off his debt. King Dave replied to Servant Phil, **"I forgive you your debt."**

Following the example of the biblical text, Servant Phil then went to Servant Olivia and demanded that she repay the debt she owed him. Just as Phil had done with King Dave, Olivia pleaded with Phil, asking for his patience and mercy. Phil knew what he was supposed to tell Olivia: that she would either pay off the debt immediately or she would be thrown into prison. But when Olivia started pleading for mercy, Phil remained silent. We waited for Phil to pronounce judgment upon Olivia but I could see his inner conflict. The more Olivia pleaded, the deeper the conflict showed on Phil's face. Finally, unable to withstand any more of Olivia's pleas, Servant Phil blurted out: **"Okay. I forgive you!"** We all had a good-natured laugh at the rewriting of the biblical text. But an unexpected insight took my breath away. I suddenly realized that I had just seen the heart of God. Phil's child-like love and his heart of compassion reflected the overwhelming desire of Abba's heart to show mercy. How can we offer anything less?

Jesus' parable substantiates his first response to Peter's question. Peter asks: "How often should I forgive my brother when he sins against me?" Jesus responds: "Always." followed by a parable which explains *why* we should forgive always. We should forgive always because Abba, in His unfathomable loving kindness, has forgiven us a debt we could **never** repay. Confronted with that magnitude of love and mercy, we will respond to others in like manner when Abba reveals to our hearts the truth of our great need and His great compassion. Like Abba, we will forgive. If we do not forgive, it is because we have not yet *"seen"* the greatness of our debt and therefore the magnitude of Abba's mercy. Our hearts have not yet been broken by Calvary's love. One thing is certain: Fear cannot make us forgive from the heart; only a revelation of Abba's love for us will conquer and soften our hearts.

Forgiveness also plays a crucial role in the quality of life on earth, not just our life in heaven. If this parable came to us without a literary context, the message would perhaps end here; i.e., "God has been so merciful to you and forgiven you a debt you could never repay, therefore you will respond by forgiving your brother's sins which are minuscule in comparison to the debt/sins God forgave you." But the parable **does** have a literary context. Something comes before it and after it. If we read Mt. 18:15-20 as part of the same context as the parable, an additional message may be noted.

Matthew 18:15 begins with the words: "If your brother sins against you. . . ." followed by the procedure for reconciling with a brother, including church discipline if necessary. Then in verse 21 Peter picks up the same phrase used by Jesus. "Lord, how often shall *my brother sin against me* and I forgive him?" The use of the same phrase is significant. It ties these passages together. In v. 15-20 the obligation of the brother who sins is to repent or else become as an outcast from the church. The church judges him. In v. 21-35 however, the obligation of the one sinned against is to forgive from the heart or else bear God's chastisement. "Yes, the church **judges** the offending brother, Peter, but you **forgive** him!" Secondly, if the sinning brother refuses to repent before the church, he is **bound** by the prayers of the church (v. 18). But if the brother sinned against refuses to forgive, he is **bound** and imprisoned by his unforgiveness (v.34). Our willingness to forgive not only affects our eternal well-being; it also affects our lives here and now. Harboring resentment and unforgiveness in our hearts will rob us of peace and joy. In extreme cases, we will be tortured by the burden (v.34).

Abba showed me that my unforgiveness (past and present) and the resulting resentment and anger not only robbed me of peace and joy but stole from me healthy relationships with others. I found I had lost much over the years due to my chains of resentment. With Abba's tender guidance, I ended up writing letters to various people for whom I harbored resentment. Some were former church members and some were family members. Some hurts and the resulting resentment stretched back into my childhood. I wrote my deceased father and forgave him for those times I wished he had been there for me. I also asked his forgiveness for my adolescent rebellion. I told him I deeply regretted the lost years and the intimate relationship we never shared. I trusted that he could either read my letter from his vantage point (heaven) or that Jesus would convey the message.

Abba's compassionate dealings with me are producing wholeness! The words "Let it go!" no longer sound ominous to my ears, but like a loving invitation from Abba to come to a place of freedom. The more I surrender to Him, the more of His life and heart He deposits within me.

Brothers and sisters, Abba loves you! He desires to show compassion and mercy to us all. He also requires us to show mercy to others, knowing that if we withhold forgiveness we will be bound in chains of our own making here in this life. We will miss His heart's desire to see us whole and free; free to love Him, others and ourselves.

Prayer: Abba, I confess that I cling to hurts and tend to nurse grudges. I now look to You for Your help and deliverance. I surrender my pains and anger to You. Free me, Abba, from the chains of my own making. Break my heart with Calvary's love and restore me to wholeness.

My Thoughts and My Prayers

Chapter 2: The Big Picture

"And we know that God causes all things to work together for good to those who love God, to those who are called according to His purpose." Romans 8:28

"After you have suffered for a little while, the God of all grace, who called you to His eternal glory in Christ will Himself perfect, confirm, strengthen and establish you." 1 Peter 5:10

"This we know–there is nothing– no circumstance, no trouble, no testing that can ever touch me until first of all it has come past God and past Christ, right through to me. If it has come that far, it has come with a great purpose which I may not understand at the moment. But as I refuse to become panicky, as I lift up my eyes to Him and accept it as coming from the throne of God for some great purpose of blessing for my own heart, no sorrow will ever destroy me, no trial will ever disarm me, no circumstance will ever cause me to give up on His faithfulness." Alan Redpath[1]

At the bottom of my pit, I wanted only one thing–OUT! I didn't want to hear a sermon on patience or a lecture on the value of trials, I simply wanted out! I refused to consider the possibility that God had anything to do with my "Katrina." I didn't want to believe that He would orchestrate or even allow such a devastating experience in my life. We can be certain that God is not the author of evil, yet in His sovereign genius and love He brings good out of evil for His children. But at my lowest point I could not appreciate any "higher purpose" in my ordeal. I could not see the big picture.

I suppose Jacob's son, Joseph, felt the same way. When God gave him those dreams of promise as a youth, I don't think he understood the process required to bring the dreams to reality. He didn't foresee jealous brothers (Joseph also ended up in a pit!), slavery or prison as part of the package, at least not while he was **in** the pit or prison. In those moments, I daresay he did not appreciate any higher purpose, he just wanted out! But young Joseph did not have the character to do the job God had ordained for him. He had to become the man God created him to be, before he could do the work God called him to do. God did have a plan for Joseph. Both the pit and the prison did have a higher purpose. Eventually, Joseph saw the hand of God in all that happened to him. Years later he told those jealous brothers who sold him into slavery, "You meant it for evil, but God meant it for good." **Joseph saw the big picture.**

At one point I remember crying out to God, "I wish this year had never taken place!" Immediately Abba reminded me of the night a few weeks earlier when He revealed to me the changes He was making in me. That night, miserable and unable to sleep, I sat in my recliner in the living room. Abba helped me see purpose in my trial. He was changing me!

He spoke to me about *my mind.* "Every thought in obedience to Christ" had become more of a reality to me than ever before. For months, there was hardly a waking moment when He was not in my thoughts and prayers. I prayed myself to sleep or prayed because I couldn't sleep. Abba was transforming my thought life and until that night, I hadn't even noticed.

He spoke to me about *my weight.* "Glorify God in your body." I had lost thirty pounds at that point and they needed to be lost. Adios and good riddance! Excess weight did not glorify God and moreover it was not the real me as Abba created me to be. My excess weight reflected an image or a label put on me by others years earlier. Now Abba was transforming me into the person He wanted me to be because He loves me. I had nothing to lose (except the pounds) and everything to gain from the transformation.

He spoke to me about *my wife.* "She is your intimate ally." The greatest transformation of all has been in my marriage. Several years earlier I purchased a book entitled *"Intimate Allies."*[2] I made the purchase because I felt my wife and I, though in the same army, were not in the same platoon. We were allies, but not **intimate allies**. She lived her life and prayed through the struggles she encountered. I lived my life and prayed through my struggles, but seldom did we come as one to God's throne. We came separately. We fought the enemy separately. Sometimes we fought one another. Truthfully, I did not think I needed her help. I purchased the book just mentioned but I never read it. I knew something was lacking in our spiritual intimacy and oneness, but I did not pursue a solution. Katrina radically changed all that. When Abba said, "She is your intimate ally," I understood the truth of His words. In the months following Katrina, my wife prayed for me constantly. She heard from God when I could not. She encouraged me day after day. She supported me and believed the best for me. She had become my intimate ally! Now we frequently sit on the couch and reflect upon our day's struggles and victories, lifting each up to Abba. We discuss those things Abba has been revealing to us. We have a time of daily prayer together at a special outdoor location near our home, then again kneeling at our children's empty beds upstairs. What a beautiful transformation Abba has made in our marriage!

Recently I officiated at a wedding. During the homily, I spoke in some detail regarding God's desire and the importance for this young couple to see their spouse as an intimate ally. I concluded with this statement: "I pray that it will not take you as many years to make that discovery as it took me." I offer that same prayer now for each of you.

Perhaps Abba has other purposes in mind besides the transformations in my life just mentioned. But even if He doesn't, I thank Him for the changes He has wrought. I praise Him for giving me a glimpse of the big picture and His loving control over my life.

Sister and brother, I don't know what kind of storm you are in, a squall or a full-blown hurricane. But I do know who has mastery over the wind and waves. I do know that Abba cares about you, loves you, and will see you through while transforming you.

Trust Abba's heart.

Prayer: O Abba, how I thank You for Your love for me! I thank You for Your faithfulness. Help me hold onto this sure foothold when all about us threatens to collapse; You love me! You have a good plan for me because Your heart is good!

The Big Picture: Making it Personal

A. Looking for something good in a "bad" situation is not natural; at least it does not come naturally to me. But Abba does not waste our experiences. If He did not orchestrate them, then He at least knew all about them before they took place. Either way, He has a loving purpose and a good plan for us just as He did for Israel. "For I know the plans that I have for you," declares the Lord, "plans for welfare and not for calamity; to give you a future and a hope." (Jer. 29:11) He is using our pits to further His good plan.

- If you have not yet seen any "good" come from your trial, ask Abba to reveal to you a positive change or changes He has made or is making in your heart and life as a result of your trial.
- Ask someone close to you what positive changes they have noted in your life as a result of your trial. Enlist them to pray with you for even greater insight into Abba's work in your life.
- Abba's deep work within us is the necessary beginning of the healing and transforming process. Our personalized trial is the door to those deep areas of our hearts needing Abba's healing touch. Invite Him to transform you into the person He created you to be so you can do the work He created you to do. Thank Him for all that He is doing in your heart and life.
- Read and meditate on the story of Joseph in Genesis chapters thirty-seven to fifty.

God of the call,
May we contemplate the good road ahead,
And walk along it,
With love in our hearts, hand in hand with you.[3]
(A Celtic prayer)

My Thoughts and Prayers

Chapter 3: The Comfort of Scripture

"This is my comfort in my affliction, that Your word has revived me." Psalm 119:50

"How sweet are Your words to my taste! Yes, sweeter than honey to my mouth!" Psalm 119:103

"I have inherited Your testimonies forever, for they are the joy of my heart." Psalm 119:111

Although I refer to the comfort of scripture as my aid in this part of my journey, I must add that I have been strengthened and sustained by scripture throughout my storm. Some of the passages mentioned here kept me from destruction before I took the first step upward. Other portions of scripture brought me further up from the pit after the journey began.

My testimony does not differ from God's people throughout the ages: His Word is a source of strength and comfort to those who are hurting. The Psalms especially offer solace. I love David's transparency! He knew how to praise God for His blessings, and he knew how to cry out to God in time of trouble. In good times and bad, David expressed his trust in the God of his salvation.

When I could not sleep I often quoted Psalm Three in my bed, emphasizing verse five in my mind; "I lay me down and I slept!" On a number of occasions I fell asleep while reciting those words of healing balm.

Psalm 40 became the theme for my wife and me throughout this period in my life. "I waited patiently for the Lord; and He inclined to me and heard my cry. He brought me up out of the pit of destruction, out of the miry clay, and He set my feet upon a rock. . . . He put a new song in my mouth, a song of praise to our God. . ." A favorite place of prayer for my wife and me has been a large rock that sits on a trail not far from our house. Naturally, we call it our "prayer rock." Many a day we have walked to the rock, sat down to pray and before leaving, stood on the rock, thanking Abba for bringing me out of the pit, setting my feet upon a rock, and putting a new song of praise in my mouth!

As with many of Abba's children, Psalm 23 repeatedly flowed through my mind. The Lord **is** my Shepherd! He really **is** leading me. He **will** take me to green pastures and still waters. He **wants** to restore my soul. He **will** get me through this valley and anoint my head. These and many other Psalms sustained me through days of despair.

At one discouraging point in my journey out of the pit, I felt Abba wanted me to read about Moses. Before I started to read, I asked Him to show me what I needed to see in that story. At the first sitting I read chapters one to fifteen of Exodus. As I read I tried to see myself in the story. How did I fit in? I asked again for Abba's wisdom and these are the thoughts that came to mind: "The message is not about you, but about me. I hear the cries of my people. I see their oppression. I know their sufferings. Pharaoh does not have the last word, I do. The Passover Lamb has been sacrificed so you can go, be free, and worship me. The horse and the rider are thrown into the sea–Rejoice! Your enemy is defeated! Jesus has conquered him and the fear of death. My children were trapped at the Red Sea. It looked impossible–Pharaoh was in pursuit. The people were frightened and cried out to Me. Moses said to them: 'Do not fear! Stand still and see the salvation of the Lord which He will accomplish for you today.'" Abba used this scripture to strengthen my heart. I not only read the passage, but I heard His still small voice speak words of encouragement to my heart personally. Abba knows how to deliver His people and that includes you!

The gospels brim with comfort for the needy. They tell the story of the God-man Jesus, the gentle Healer. From His heart of love and compassion He goes about doing good. He heals the sick, cleanses lepers, weeps with those who weep and heals the broken-hearted. At the outset of His earthly ministry He quotes Isaiah 61 as His standing orders, His reason for being sent to earth.

> The Spirit of the Lord is upon Me, because He anointed Me to preach the gospel to the poor. He has sent Me to proclaim release to the captives, and recovery of sight to the blind, to set free those who are oppressed, to proclaim the favorable year of the Lord.

Jesus did what He saw the Father doing. His heart of love and compassion reflect the heart of His Father. When Jesus wept with pity, Abba's heart was also breaking. When Jesus rejoiced over a sinner made whole, the heart of Abba was rejoicing also (see Luke 15, for example).

I saw the heart of Jesus as I read The Song of Solomon. Solomon's song primarily describes the love and sensual attraction between Solomon and his bride-to-be. But as many have testified, past and present, this song might also reflect the love between Jesus and His bride. In my hour of need, I became the bride and Jesus the groom. As I read this song I first noticed the great love, desire and admiration of the bride for her beloved. She can't wait to be kissed, for his love is better than wine (better than any substitute, chemical or otherwise) (1:2). The bride longs to find the one whom her soul loves. "Tell me, O you whom my soul loves, where do you pasture your flock. . .?" (1:7) She eagerly anticipates his arrival, she can't wait to see him. "Listen! My beloved! Behold, he is coming, climbing on the mountains." (2:8) When she does find him, she will not let go of him. (3:4) The bride knows nothing but the highest praise and admiration for the attributes of her beloved. "My beloved is dazzling and ruddy, outstanding among ten thousand. His head is like gold, pure gold. . . .His mouth is full of sweetness, and he is wholly desirable. This is my beloved and this is my friend. . ." (5:9-16) Yes, I believed the bride's love and admiration for the groom well-justified. I saw Jesus, my Lord, in the same, albeit spiritual light.

As I read the Song of Solomon, I could easily identify with the bride's attraction and love for her groom, but a more amazing idea surfaced: the Groom, the King, likewise is enthralled with His beloved! He wants intimacy with her. He draws her to Himself (1:4). He extends His hand to her (5:4). He is looking for her through the window (2:9) and knocking at her door (5:2). He wants to see her and hear her voice (2:14). The King also tells His bride that **her** love is better than wine (4:10). Yes, I could easily identify with the bride's love and desire for the groom, but the love and desire which the groom has for the bride touched my heart. Jesus assured me that He **is** the lover of my soul and that His love mirrors perfectly the love of Abba's heart.

I felt I should read and meditate upon the Gospel account of the paralytic in Mark 2:1-12. I slowly and prayerfully read the account a number of times. At one point, I saw myself as the paralytic. His thoughts, his hopes and his fears seemed to become mine. I recorded the following dramatization of Mark 2:1-12 in my prayer journal:

Jesus is at home! He is gone so much and I cannot be carried to other cities or into the mountains in search of Him. But now, the rumor spreads like wildfire throughout the streets of our town: "He's home!"

I am excited and hopeful! "Hurry, let's go," I tell my friends, "before He leaves again." I want to walk so badly. This is my chance! Maybe today I'll see Jesus and He will heal me. My four friends carefully transfer me from my bed to a pallet on which to transport me. All five of us feel something strange, almost foreign, in the depths of our beings. It is buoyant; something bubbling and effervescent lightens and lifts our hearts. We feel HOPE! We approach His house. So many people! We are not the only ones who want to see and hear the Master. A great crowd is packed into the house and overflowing to the street outside. At least we know the rumors are true, He **is** at home. We are just yards away from Him. Only a wall of mud bricks and a wall of people separate me from the One whom I so desperately want and need to see. But we are too late. How will I ever get inside to see Him? My hope quickly vanishes. I will never make it through the crowd into Jesus' Presence. He will never know that I am outside longing to see Him, and when He leaves, I will not be able to follow.

A desperate idea penetrates our minds, as though it were inserted there from without. Almost as one we shout, "The roof!" We cannot make a new doorway in the wall, but the roof can be breached without special tools. One friend runs to get rope. After returning, two friends climb to the roof while the other two lift my pallet, with me on it, up to our waiting compatriots. Now all on the roof, we start digging a hole about 7 feet long and 3 feet wide at a spot we calculate would be right above where Jesus is sitting below. I am more a hindrance than a help, but that doesn't bother anyone. Now only a few feet and some mud separate me from Jesus! We dig with a heart! Soon, a gaping hole stares at us. Covered with mud and sweat, we look down and see that Jesus is still where we had hoped He would be. Hallelujah!

My friends each stand at a corner of the hole and start to lower me through the roof with the ropes. I am excited, yet also frightened. What will Jesus do when He sees me? What will He say to me? Will He let me plead for my healing? Will He even speak to me? Will He be angry because of the roof? Being lowered through the roof is eerie, kind of like being lowered into a grave. At first I can see no one, but then a little lower and I see people standing shoulder to shoulder. They move back so I do not land on their heads. I can't see Jesus—where is He? Now suspended only a few feet off the floor, I look to my left and there, within arm's length, sits Jesus. I look at Him, wanting to pour out my plea and beg Him to heal me, but when I see His face, the words retreat from my lips. I don't know what to think. Jesus is looking up at the hole in His roof and gazing at my four friends. He is smiling!

By now I am on the floor at Jesus' feet, waiting for I know not what. Jesus looks down at me with the most tender eyes I have ever seen. He speaks five words to me. Five words that have changed my life: "Child, your sins are forgiven." They are not the words I expected, nor the words I wanted to hear, yet as they are spoken I feel a wave of peace wash over me. My paralyzed heart feels warm and malleable as never before. Though I cannot yet walk, I can now love and receive love. I understand by some new-found instinct that Jesus has chosen to speak to me with a view to true priorities. More than anything else in this life or the next, I need to become a forgiven child of God with a heart made whole. But to be honest, as thankful as I am to be forgiven and renewed in my heart, I still want to walk!

While I ponder His words, Jesus turns His attention to the lawyers who are offended by His words to me. If those lawyers only knew what happened to me, they would have wanted Jesus to speak the same words to them! But at this point, they do not see themselves as having any such need of forgiveness. Did I hear Jesus' final words to the lawyers correctly; something about a paralytic walking? Then He looks at me again with those eyes from which nothing is hid. He gazes into my eyes. His voice grows noticeably softer, like being caressed with words. He speaks the words my new heart longs to hear: "I say to you, get up, and pick up your pallet. You can go home now." Before the words are out of His mouth, I feel my useless legs bursting with life and strength. I could not lie there another second! It feels like I am being pushed off my pallet. I gladly comply with the command; up I jump! I pick up my former means of conveyance and I got a-skipping home to the amazement of all who see me.

On that day my life changed forever. I can now walk and work and provide for my family; but even more importantly, I can love. Glory to our God and to His Son, Jesus the Messiah, my Savior. I was lowered down and Jesus raised me up! Hallelujah!

Prayer: Abba, how I thank you for the testimony of Your word! Through it the Spirit bears witness of Your amazing love for me; a truth made crystal clear through Jesus Christ, my Lord. Continue to speak Your words of resurrection life to my heart. From the depths of my pit, raise me up and renew my heart with Your love. "Jesus loves me this I know, for the Bible tells me so."

Scripture: Making it Personal

A. Lectio divina (sacred reading) is an ancient method of reading and meditating upon Scripture. With this approach to Bible reading, we are not analyzing Scripture with our minds, but allowing the Spirit to speak to our hearts from the words of the Bible. The primary goal in lectio divina is not to intellectually dissect a passage, but to encounter and hear from Jesus in our hearts. His words are more than a source for doctrinal statements; they are also spirit and life when quickened to our hearts by the Spirit.

During my journey out of the pit, Abba has been teaching me to use this right-brained method of Bible reading in addition to the more analytical approach I had been accustomed to. The Gospel account of the paralytic in Mark 2:1-12 mentioned above is one such example of the meditative approach.

- Ask Jesus to lead you to a passage He would have you meditate upon. There are a number of books to help you with this method such as Richard Foster's *Prayer: Finding the Heart's True Home*. To begin with, you may want to follow this spiritual director's advice found in Foster's book (paraphrased): "Go to the passage and be open to receive whatever God has for you. Don't manipulate God; just receive . . . open your Bible, read it slowly, listen to it, and reflect on it."[4]

  The goal is to experience Jesus in our reading, perhaps as one of the characters in the account, or maybe by hearing the Spirit speak to us through the words we read.
  Use a journal or the following page to record whatever you receive from Jesus.

My Thoughts and My Prayers

Chapter 4: A Blade of Mordor

"The serpent said to the woman, "Hath God said. . . .? You surely will not die! (if you eat the fruit) For God knows that in the day you eat from it your eyes will be opened. . ." Genesis 3:4,5

"You are of your father the devil . . . there is no truth in him. Whenever he speaks the lie, he speaks from his own nature, for he is a liar and the father of lies." John 8:44

"He who has received His (Jesus') testimony has set his seal to this, that God is true." John 3:33

". . . be on the alert. Your adversary, the devil, prowls around . . . seeking someone to devour. But resist him, stand firm in faith. . ." 1 Peter 5:8, 9

We have an enemy! He cannot take us from Abba's hand, nor can he force us to do evil. If he could do either, we would no longer belong to Abba and the world would only be filled with evil. Our enemy's chief weapons are lies and deception. At one point on my journey out of the pit, I continually felt a heaviness of spirit, an oppression I could not shake, even after Abba had helped me in so many ways. My wife and I both had the idea to call our friends John and Debra who live two hours away. They are pastors involved in healing ministry both at the local church level and beyond. We called and made what turned out to be a divine appointment. I first told them the entire account of my "Katrina." I told them about the "knife in the gut" and much more. I withheld nothing. I then related how Abba had been bringing me out of the pit but not without ongoing struggles. After a time of waiting on the Lord, both John and Debra sensed that there was still some poison within me; as though a tip of the blade had broken off inside me. Immediately Frodo Baggins came to mind.

You probably recognize the name of the central character of J.R.R Tolkien's *Lord of the Rings Trilogy*.[5] Early in the adventure, Frodo, who carries a prize dear to the dark lord of Mordor, is stabbed with a knife by a servant of the dark lord. The wound itself is not deep, but it is deadly. The knife used is a blade of Mordor, cursed with evil and able to kill one's spirit and eventually the body. Thankfully for Frodo, there is a master-healer not too distant who removes the poisonous piece of knife from his body.

The poison remaining in me could be named fear, anxiety, discouragement and even despair. Everyone has fears, anxieties, and becomes discouraged, but mine was a heaviness that I could not shake. This was not just an emotional response to my wound, but a spiritual battle which required spiritual weapons to combat. So, we fought.

I laid my heart open before these friends and Abba, confessing my sins and the sins of my ancestors which still affected me. John and Debra prayed healing prayers over me, anointing me with oil and praying that Jesus would set me free from my past and the brokenness passed down to me by my forefathers. We praised Abba for His great mercy and mighty deliverance. We shared the Lord's Supper at His table. With Abba's help, I fought (and still fight) the enemy with truth.

As mentioned, the enemy's chief weapon is the lie. He used it against Eve and he used against me. He has used it against you. "Hath God said. . . ? You cannot trust God! His motives are questionable. He doesn't really have your best interests at heart. He really does not care about you!" (my paraphrase of Genesis 3:1-5) My fears and anxieties and discouragement were all based upon lies that I had believed. Lies the enemy whispered to me about Abba; e.g., "God is not really trustworthy. He does not really love you; He just wants to use you. In the big picture, you are insignificant to Him. If you were really important to God, you wouldn't be going through this!" The lies had taken root in me, but Jesus said, "The truth shall set you free!" What is the truth according to Jesus? **God is TRUE!** (John 3:33) He does not just speak truth, but He is TRUE. There is **nothing** false about Him. We can "set our seal to it." In other words, we can take it to the bank. We can count on it. We can put our full weight on this irrevocable truth: God is TRUE! Every word He speaks, every motive, every thought, and in every dealing with us, He is TRUE. When all else fails, if everyone else forsakes us or betrays us or rejects us, we can count on this: Abba is trustworthy! There is no guile or shadow in Him. Abba's heart is pure and we can trust Him.

When we left John and Debra's the next day, I was not entirely whole; discouragement and anxiety still raised their ugly heads from time to time. By no means am I an expert on spiritual warfare, but the Master-healer removed the poisonous tip of Mordor's blade and helped me take a noticeable step upward. Our time with these friends also helped prepare me for my next step– Silent Week.

Prayer: Dear Abba, I repent for those times I have believed the lie about You; when I have doubted You, Your goodness and Your love for me. Please forgive me! Thank you for Your perfect heart; perfectly pure, kind, and full of mercy. Thank you that there is one thing I can count on though all else may fail; You are TRUE! Help me trust you, I pray. In Jesus' blessed Name.

A Blade of Mordor: Making It Personal

A. We have all inherited Adam's sinful nature (Romans 5). Besides inheriting Adam's sinful nature in general, it is possible that we inherit or acquire specific sins from our parents who in turn inherited those same sins from their parents, and so on. These "family" sins are frequently learned behaviors that children quickly "pick up on" when young, then make them their own as they grow older. Some examples of inherited sins are: great anger, alcoholism, infidelity, habitual lying, sexual perversion, gluttony, perfectionism and many more. Although the sinful pattern is often learned behavior, it can easily take on "a life of its own." When specific sins become "embedded" into a family for generations, they acquire a spiritual identity and power beyond just a learned behavior. I do not mean to imply that all children will inevitably be bound by their family's sins, but **everyone** is affected. Spiritual strongholds of sin can be broken by the Holy Spirit. As Christians, we are empowered by the Spirit of God to "put to death the deeds of the flesh." (Romans 8:13) This work of the Spirit is an ongoing process in our lives.

- If you believe you are ensnared or bound by a specific sin or sins that you have not been able to overcome, especially sins that seem to "run in the family," you may want to pray the following prayer.

  Dear Abba, I ask forgiveness for my ancestors, including my parents, for sins of anger, bitterness, alcohol and drug abuse, sexual sins, and violence (add any other sins you deem applicable). In addition to forgiveness for my ancestors, I pray that you forgive me for embracing those sins. I repent of my willing acceptance and practice of habitual sins and I ask for Your help and grace to forgive those who have sinned against me. I pray that You break the power those sins have over me and my children. In the name of Jesus Christ and by the power of His blood and His resurrection, I now cut off all generational sins and the consequences of those sins that are preventing me and my children from living the life You have created me (us) to live. In Jesus' name, I break and make null and void any expression of evil sent against me or passed down to me or my children. Thank You, Lord Jesus, for Your presence in my life. May Your love and forgiveness continue to draw me and my children into places of peace and wholeness.

B. If there were a single core truth revealed in the Bible, I believe it would be that Abba loves you so much that **He sent His Son to die for you**. That act of love was prophesied in the Old Testament and fulfilled in the New Testament. Paul asks the question, "If God is **for** us, who can be against us? **He who did not spare His own Son**, but delivered Him over for us all . . . ." (Romans 8: 32,33) Jesus told His followers that it would not be necessary for Him (Jesus) to make requests to His Abba on our behalf, because ". . . the Father Himself loves you. . ." (John 16:27) Abba **loves** you and is **for** you, not against you!

- The enemy of our souls continually tries to cast doubt on the love and character of Abba. When our plans don't seem to work out, Satan says, "God doesn't love you!" When we receive bad news the enemy whispers "You can't trust God!" Evil things do happen in this world. That is certain. But just as certain is the fact that Abba is not the author of evil, Satan is. Do not believe the words of "the liar and the father of lies," (i.e., Satan, John 8) but trust and believe the One who died for you!

- In your prayer journal or on the following page, tell Abba if you have believed the enemy's lies about Him. Confess your doubts. He will not be upset because you tell Him the truth. He already knows the truth about us and still loves us! Ask Him to open the eyes of your heart so you can see the boundless love He has for you. Ask Him to open your inner ear so you can hear the words of love He is speaking to you.

- Pray this personalized prayer found in Ephesians 3:14-21:

> *I bow my knees before You, Abba, and pray that You would grant me, according to the riches of Your glory, to be strengthened with power through Your Spirit in my inner man, so that Christ Jesus may dwell in my heart through faith; that I, being rooted and grounded in love, may be able to comprehend with all the saints what is the breadth and length and height and depth, and to know the love of Christ for me which surpasses knowledge; that I may be filled up to all the fullness of God. Now to You who are able to do far more abundantly beyond all that I ask or think, according to the power that works within me, to You be the glory in the church and in Christ Jesus to all generations forever and ever. Amen.*

My Thoughts and My Prayers

Chapter 5: Silent Week

"Then they sat down on the ground with him for seven days and seven nights with no one speaking a word to him, for they saw that his pain was very great." Job 2:13

"I literally willed myself to sit down with my prayer journal and pour my heart out to God. . . allowing the release of what was in my heart so I could receive what was in His heart."[6] Signa Bodishbaugh

I don't know exactly *how* I knew Abba wanted me to be silent for one week, but I knew. The concept was not new to me. I had read and heard of others who practiced silence for a designated length of time, but I never thought I would be one of them! The plan was conceived before our visit to John and Debra's. Through my experience with our friends, Abba confirmed the plan. I would commence my "silent week" the following Sunday evening at 6 PM.

Only my wife and children knew about the plan before the event took place. My daughter, Erin, called me at 5:45 PM that Sunday to pray for me. One item she mentioned in her prayer was that God already had the curriculum picked out for me during this week. She was exactly right! Several books I had finished just prior to my week were instrumental in my preparation: E. Stanley Jones' *A Song of Ascents* (see endnotes #8), and Hannah W. Smith's *The Christian's Secret of a Happy Life* (see endnotes #11). (Stanley Jones mentioned Hannah Smith's book as being influential in his own life). Another book was helpful in the week following the silence; *Wild at Heart* by John Eldredge.[7] I am amazed how these books dovetailed together to form a focused message to me from Abba.

During my silent week, God provided two main text books for me (other than the Bible). The first book sovereignly and literally "dropped into my lap" at 3 PM on that Sunday; the title: *The Journey to Wholeness in Christ*, a 40 day devotional by Signa

Bodishbaugh (see endnote #6). The other book was titled *Abba's Child* by Brennan Manning.[8] These two books were marvelously used of Abba to bring me closer in intimacy and therefore to wholeness in Him during the week.

My home was my monastery for silent week. My wife was gone for much of each day. We never spoke, but when necessary we communicated through hand signals or by notes for more complicated messages. I only left the house two times a day; once every morning for a walk by myself in the woods, and again in the early evening with my wife. Both walks followed the same path and ended at the same "prayer rock" where I/we would pray silently. We planned the route and the routine the day before my silent week began.

My goal at the outset during this difficult period of my life was to draw near to God and for Him to draw near to me. I think what I really wanted, but was afraid to articulate, was to **know** that God loved me! I did not feel loved. I wanted and needed an intimacy with Him that I had never known or at least I had forgotten. I needed an experience, a **real** knowing, not just a theological teaching.

I commenced this week with a prayer written in my prayer journal in the form of a letter to Abba:

> *I want to come spend some time alone with you—just You and me! I want to share my joys and sorrows with you; I want to hear Your words of advice and wise counsel. I would also like to hear what is on Your heart, things You want to share with me. But mostly, I just want to be with you; to let you know how much I appreciate You and the great dad you are and have been, even when I wasn't that great of a son. I regret*

that I haven't spent more time alone with You, but I'm looking forward to making up for lost time!

With love from Your son,
Owen

Abba taught me two great truths during my silent week. The first I refer to as my "great discovery." A month prior to silent week, a pastor-friend told me he had been praying for me. God had shown him that I would make a great discovery. In the picture God gave him, he saw (as a type) gold miners striking a rich vein of gold ore–a monumental discovery. I would also make a tremendous discovery he assured me. I prayed for weeks that God would show me the discovery He had for me. My discovery came during my silent week. I struck GOLD! I discovered that I am Abba's Child! I am His beloved son. He is my Papa who not only loves me but wants what is best for me. He wants me to hear His voice of tenderness and healing love. He wants an intimate relationship with me more than I could possibly imagine. Yes, I knew all of this in theory and I believed it prior to silent week. I can only say, the reality of my great discovery ushered in a closeness, a warmth and an intimate communion with Abba I had never known.

There can be no doubt that Abba wants this and more for you! He longs for intimacy with you! He desires your wholeness because you are His child and His love for you will never falter or end. This is true regardless of our pits. It is true even when it does not feel like the truth. Abba would not have sent His Son for us unless He loved us with a greater love than we can fathom.

The second truth learned during silent week was "surrender." Abba's love and my surrender became the warp and woof of the week. He knit the two together in perfect harmony. How did He unite these two truths? First He assured me that He loved me, then He showed me what I needed to surrender to Him in order to become whole. Only when I became certain of and secure in His love, was I willing to surrender myself and my "baggage" to Him. I surrendered sins, fears, resentments, hurts, brokenness, and the list goes on. Many of those things surrendered had to be unearthed by Abba once I opened my heart to Him. They were buried deep in my past and needed to be exposed by someone who loved me unconditionally and for the purpose of helping me. I needed someone I could trust implicitly; that someone was Abba.

E. Stanley Jones wrote about the apostles of ill health; attitudes like: anger, resentment, fear, worry, and jealousy. He concluded that prayer is primarily self-surrender with no strings attached; but also it is a day-by-day surrender of our problems, attitudes included.[9] Every time I surrendered something unhealthy in my heart, I asked Abba to replace it with some good thing from His heart. I surrendered despair and He replaced it with hope. I surrendered resentment and he replaced it with peace. I surrendered my fear of abandonment and He exchanged it with His assurance that He will never leave me. Rejection and the fear of abandonment critically hindered my surrender to Abba for years. The same fear cripples many of our spiritual lives. Henri Nouwen writes:

> As soon as someone accuses me or criticizes me, as soon as I am rejected, left alone, or abandoned, I find myself thinking, 'Well, that proves once again that I am a nobody.' My dark side says I am no good, I deserve to be pushed aside, forgotten, rejected. Self-rejection is the greatest enemy of the spiritual life because it contradicts the sacred voice that calls us the 'beloved.' Being the beloved constitutes the core truth of our existence."[10]

I am overjoyed to report to you that I am Abba's child! I am His beloved son. He is my Papa who not only loves me but wants what is best for me. He wants me to hear His voice of tenderness and healing love. He also wants my total surrender, to trust Him with my life, my future, and my heart. I am also overjoyed to report the same is true for YOU! You are Abba's child. You are His beloved. He wants to speak words of healing love to you and He wants your surrendered heart. Dear friends, you can trust Abba! You are precious in His sight. Offer Him your brokenness and watch with wonder as He replaces it with something good from His heart.

Prayer: Dear Abba. I confess there are times when I question Your love for me. I know it is not right and I feel guilty for my doubts, but it's the truth. Abba, I surrender my doubts to You. I surrender my fears to You. Please take them from my heart and replace them with good things from Your heart. Help me *hear* the words of healing love You are speaking to me. Thank You, Abba! In Jesus' blessed name I pray.

Silence/Solitude: Making it Personal

A. In order to hear Abba's voice, we must be still and listen. Because of many demands upon you, you may not be able to practice silence and solitude for seven consecutive days or even seven consecutive hours, yet finding some amount of "quiet time" is vital.

- Pray for Abba's help to discover what will work best for you. Perhaps you can wake up a half hour earlier or use a portion of your lunch hour to spend time alone with Abba. Though it may seem like a sacrifice, you will soon relish these times of intimacy, communion and fellowship with Abba and Jesus.
- There are a number of good books to help you develop an intimate prayer life. I have found Richard Foster's *Prayer, Finding the Heart's True Home* [11] very helpful.

B. Surrender and Receive: Jesus frequently used agricultural concepts for His parables: seeds, gardens, fields, wheat, tares, etc. In Mark 4, Jesus tells a parable describing various problems which prevent His word form bearing fruit in our hearts and lives. Some things, like weeds, choke Jesus' word so it has no positive impact in our lives. Weeds might represent worries of the world, the deceitfulness of riches, harmful habits, and other unhealthy desires.

During my silent week, Abba clearly showed me weeds in my life that He wanted me to surrender to Him. One such weed was television. I spent far too much time watching TV and videos. That addiction not only wasted a great amount of time, but also polluted my heart and mind with unwholesome words, images, and attitudes. I knew Abba wanted me to surrender my evenings to Him, especially the hours wasted watching TV. In its place, He has given my wife and me a blessed time of prayer and communion. He has exchanged my need for vicarious excitement and stimulation with real-life adventures beyond which I could have imagined.

- In prayer, open your heart and soul to Abba. Ask Him to show you what weeds are choking His word in your heart and hindering His plan for your life. Surrender those weeds and visualize Jesus pulling them out by their roots. Pray that Abba replace what you surrender with something good and life-giving from His heart, plantings that will bear much good fruit.

My Thoughts and My Prayers

Chapter 6: How Much More

"If you then, being evil, know how to give good gifts to your children, how much more will your Father who is in heaven give what is good to those who ask Him!" Matthew 7:11

"Consider the ravens, for they neither sow nor reap; they have neither storeroom nor barn, and yet God feeds them; how much more valuable you are than the birds!" Luke 12:24

"And Jesus said, 'Truly I say to you, unless you are converted and become like children, you will not enter the kingdom of heaven.'" Matthew 18:3

"The life of faith, then, about which I am writing, consists in just this–being a child in the Father's house."[12] Hannah Whitall Smith

When I began my "silent week," I did not address God as "Abba." I typically used the term "Father" when praying to God. Suddenly, on the third day of my silent week, my prayers and indeed, my relationship with the Father entered a new dimension. I simply think of the transformation as a result of Abba revealing to me the "how much more" principle.

To illustrate the sudden transformation, I include the prayer from my journal moments before the change. "**Father**, is there anything else You want me to 'see' or grasp from my reading? Is there anything else You want to show me or say to me?" I used the term "Father" as I normally did. Allow me to interject here that I would not have normally (prior to silent week) asked such an open-ended question of God and expected any kind of detailed answer coming from Him as a direct response to my question. I simply followed along with Signa Bodishbaugh as she led me on *The Journey to Wholeness*. I tried to put into practice the ideas she lay before me. She writes:

> We will read God's word every day. We will open
> our hearts to Him in prayer in a quiet place. We will
> listen for His healing personal word to us. We will
> keep a listening prayer journal. We will try to obey
> what He tells us to do, knowing that He will
> empower us to do far more than we are able to do in
> our own strength.[13]

After asking Father if there was anything else He wanted to
say to me, I then waited quietly, listening for His voice with pen and
journal in hand. I confess I was not sure what to expect next, but
what my heart heard transformed my relationship with God. At that
time in my life my heart was filled with thoughts about our youngest
daughter whose wedding would take place one month later. God
answered my prayer like this:

> Just as your daughter, Gwendolyn, is precious to you,
> you are precious to me! Just as you want the best for
> Gwendolyn, I want the best for you! Just as you long
> to hear her voice, to welcome her into your presence
> and your embrace, so I long to hear from you, to
> welcome you into my presence, and my embrace!

From that moment on, I have addressed my personal prayers
to "Papa," an English equivalent to the Aramaic "Abba." I did not
plan for that change. I did not sit down and calculate with what title
I should address God. When I heard His response, the cry of my
heart was, "Oh Papa!"(the same name used by my children when
they address me, personally). I immediately bore my soul to Him.
"Oh Papa, it has been a hard year for me! I have been betrayed and
rejected. . . I have been deeply hurt; I have wallowed in self-pity and
self-preoccupation; I have been sick, discouraged and despairing,
but You have also comforted and encouraged me. Thank You! Papa,
You have always been there for me."

Abba loves all He created, including birds, flowers and people. Jesus used the "how much more" principle to encourage His disciples to trust Abba. If God feeds the birds, *how much more* will He care for you? (Luke 12:24) You are more valuable than birds! Also, if a human father cares for his children and wants good things for them; if a human father with all his limitations and sinful tendencies loves his children, *how much more* does the heavenly Father love *His* children and want good things for them?(Mt. 7:11)

I love my children! Now that they are all grown, I love when they return home. I love when they want to spend time with me. When the children were younger, I would often walk with them on trails in the woods around our home. This is especially true of our son, Elijah. We would hike. We would play hide and seek with our dog. We named certain locations in the woods with our own "secret" code names. Soon after hearing Abba's words, I took a walk in the same woods as I had with my son throughout his childhood. I suddenly knew that Abba wanted to be invited to go with me! Just as I am delighted when my grown son says to me, "Papa, let's go for a hike like we used to do;" so was Abba delighted to be asked to accompany me on my hike. If I, a human father, long to spend time with my son, and am moved to tears of joy to know he wants to spend time with me, just *me*, **HOW MUCH MORE** does Abba delight when I want to spend time with Him!

Abba longs for close and intimate communion with you. He wants to hear your voice. He longs to spend time with you, more than you want to spend time with your child or your dearest friend or your spouse. He wants to speak His personal and loving words to your heart. He wants you to be whole! Whatever the equivalent to a "bear hug" is in heaven, that's what Abba wants to give you. Come to Him like a child and you will thrill His heart. Run to His arms and let Him wrap you in His warm embrace. As He holds you, you will know the love of Abba's heart. As you continue in times of intimacy with Abba, you will discover that you are being transformed into the person He created you to be–a whole person.

Prayer: Oh Abba! It sounds too simple, too child-like; that I not only can run to You and share my deepest secrets with You, but You *want me* to do so! I can come without fear of rejection, but with a certainty that I am always welcome into Your presence, more than I would welcome my own beloved children. Thank You for Your love for me which is higher and deeper and broader than any love I have ever known. Amen.

How Much More: Making it Personal

A. Letter writing:

- If you have a child, take a few minutes to write him/her a love letter. Use whatever greeting that expresses your love, followed by your child's name. For example: *My Dearest Daughter Sally.* In your letter, express your heart's great love in your own words. Perhaps you have spoken or written these words in the past to your child, or maybe you've never been able to express them. Conclude your letter with a closing that reflects your love. For example: *With all my love, mom.* If you have no biological children, compose your letter to any child or young person with whom you are especially close. Please complete this exercise before reading on.

- In the Old Testament, God is rarely referred to as "Father." Occasionally, He refers to Himself as the Father of the nation of Israel, but there is not any record of an individual walking around and addressing God as "Father" in the Old Testament. One reason the religious leaders of Jesus day were so offended by Him, was due to the fact that He continually referred to God as His Father, a revolutionary idea which many considered heretical (John 5:18). But Jesus not only called God **His** Father, He also told His disciples that God was **their** Father! For example, in the Lord's Prayer, Jesus taught His disciples to pray: "**Our** Father who is in heaven. . ." (Mt. 6:9ff); and Luke 12:30, ". . . but **your** Father knows. . ." or in John 20:17 Jesus tells Mary to convey this message to His disciples: "I ascend to My Father and **your** Father. . ." The idea becomes even more radical when Paul declares that God is not only our Father, but our "Abba, Father!" (Romans 8:15) i.e., our intimate, loving, sit-on-His-lap and snuggle kind of Father–our daddy or our Papa!

- Refer now to the above letter-writing exercise. That
exercise was not primarily for the purpose of sending
your letter to your child, although that would be fine. But
first I would like you, at least mentally, to replace your
child's name, wherever you wrote it, with your own.
Next, replace your name at the end of the letter with the
name, "Abba." This letter is now addressed to you and
sent from Abba. Reread your letter as though you were
the recipient. Perhaps not every detail will apply to you,
but in whatever words you expressed your heart's love to
your child, you can rest assured that they also reflect
Abba's love for you. In truth, our words of love to our
children are but a dim reflection of Abba's love for them
and us. **"How much more"** does He love us!

B. Abba and Jesus want an intimate relationship with us. They want
to share the same love they have for one another with us. (John
17:23, 26) Experiencing their intimate love will transform our lives.
One of the most intimate moments between Jesus and His twelve
disciples occurred during the last Passover when Jesus washed His
disciples' feet. (John 13)

- Read John 13:1-12. After reading the passage, visualize
the scene with the eyes of your heart as though you were
present in the upper room. Jesus arises from the table and
walks to the end of the room. No one questions His
actions at this point. Then He removes His outer
garments and tucks a towel into His waistband. Now the
disciples, quite perplexed, look at one another and mouth
the words, *"What's going on?"* Jesus takes a pitcher of
water and fills a basin. *"What's He doing with the
water?"* the disciples ponder. Jesus brings the towel and
basin of water and stands before the nearest disciple. No
one understands, but everyone senses that something

unprecedented is about to happen. Just then, Jesus kneels before the first disciple's feet. A wave of disbelief stuns the disciples into silence. Each heart shouts out: *"What is He doing?!"* *"You can't do that, Jesus!"* Peter finally vocalizes what all are thinking. *"You will not wash my feet!"* But He does. He kneels before those whom He created and washes the feet He Himself crafted (John 1:3). Visualize Jesus gently picking up the feet of every disciple, one by one. Holding each soiled foot with one hand, He tenderly washes away dirt, mud, bruises, and weariness. Then, He takes the towel and lovingly dries their feet. He repeats this act twenty-four times for those whom He intimately loves, including His betrayer.

- I would like you to visualize the same scene again. Jesus is with His disciples, a basin of water in His hands and a towel at His waist. This time, however, picture Him kneeling before you! He is tenderly holding your feet, one at a time. With one hand, He holds your foot, and with His other hand He gently washes it. Can you feel the energy of His love flowing through you as He holds your foot? What is He washing from you? Visualize Him looking at you and speaking to you. What is He saying to you? With the ears of your heart, listen for His words of intimate love.

My Thoughts and My Prayers

Chapter 7: Having Done All to Stand, Stand

"Therefore, take up the full armor of God, so that you will be able to resist in the evil day, and having done everything to stand, stand firm." (Ephesians 6:13)

"Moses said to the people, 'Do not fear! Stand still and see the salvation of the Lord which He will accomplish for you today. . .'" (Exodus 14:13)

I knew I could not extricate myself from the pit. My testimony echoes David's: "*He* brought me up out of the pit. . . ." (Psalm 40:2) Paul encourages the Ephesians to ". . . be strong in the Lord and in the strength of **His** might." (Ephesians 6:10) Just three verses later however, Paul exhorts his readers to "stand firm." (Eph. 6:13) Even though there can be no doubt that Abba was lifting me out of my pit, He did expect my willing cooperation and obedience; "having done all to stand, stand firm." At this point in my journey out of the pit, I didn't know what else to do. I had surrendered to Abba everything I knew to surrender to the best of my ability. I had confessed every sin and sinful attitude He had revealed to me up to that point. I asked forgiveness from those whom I had resented. I forgave those who had wronged me. I sought Him, by His own instruction and enabling grace, during a silent week. None of this was done flawlessly, but I hoped it was all done sincerely. Having done all I knew to do (through His strength), I now awaited the next step to wholeness. I could not have predicted Abba's next move.

We attended a church with friends of ours. It was our first Sunday worship experience with them. I noted in the bulletin an invitation to any who desired "healing prayers" to come for prayer after the morning service. A team of trained brothers and sisters would be happy to pray for anyone interested. I was definitely interested! I met with the five-member team after the service. I gave them a bare-bones description of my problem which had a spiritual, emotional and physical dimension to it. They began to pray. Their prayers touched my heart; they were sincere and heart-felt. Then Judy, a lively dynamo of a senior citizen and a member of the prayer team, started to pray. She prayed with authority, but also with God-given insight. It was as though she had been reading my prayer journal! Her words had the distinct tone of Abba's voice in them. She said: "Having done all to stand, stand! Stand still and watch God's deliverance. The burden of the battle is no longer yours. Abba removes it from your back. (She and others enacted those words by removing the invisible but very real burden from my back). Just stand still and watch God take out His sword and cut you free." At this point, she wielded an invisible sword and made great swaths with it around my kneeling form. Judy had no idea that she quoted nearly verbatim the scripture promises Abba had given me during my silent week; "Stand still and see the salvation of God . . ." She had no idea the weight of the burden I carried. As she prayed, I wept.

Within a week, I noted a definite "lifting" of my spirit and an improvement in my physical symptoms. I had no doubt that Abba was "cutting me free." In the weeks following, I noted that as part of His sword-work He sent others to speak to me and pray for me. At least one person every week came to minister to me and through them Abba cut asunder more chains.

Our three children returned home for several days. As we all sat on the couch, they offered up prayers for me, their papa. Their prayers saturated me with a healing balm and strengthened me anew.

- "Dear Lord, turn Papa's gaze just 45 degrees so he is not looking at the timing of Your restoration, but directly at You!"
- "Dear Lord, put a new song of praise in Papa's mouth."
- "O Lord, show Papa what a privilege it is to

suffer with Christ Jesus."
- "Dear Father, make a new creation in Papa and give him a Sabbath rest in You. Although we can no longer touch the hem of Jesus' garment, Jesus would you reach down to touch Papa."

Abba used these prayers and others like them to cut me free of the chains that bound me.

Then Abba sent Melba, a dear friend whom we had not seen for some years. She is a chaplain and counselor. She provided helpful reading material, sound advice, clarifying insights and a ton of experience. Above all, she kept probing my heart for unhealed wounds then *listened* to me.

The week following my first meeting with Melba, Abba sent a praying married couple across my path. As we spent time praying in Abba's presence, I saw with greater clarity how my childhood relationships, especially with my father and mother, affected my relationships with others, especially my own wife and children. The prayers offered for me that night, and those that poured from my own heart, loosed another binding chain and brought me closer to wholeness.

On this journey with Abba, He will send you helpers along the way to succor, strengthen and pray for you. But He will also ask you to cooperate with Him in specific ways. Everything He asks of you will clearly benefit you. His grace will allow you to accomplish what He asks of you. He has your best interest at heart! When you have done all, stand. And then watch what Abba will do! (Exodus 6:1)

Prayer: Dear Abba, thank You for sending me those who will encourage and support me with love and prayer during these days of hardship. But also help me listen for Your guiding voice as You lead me and help me cooperate in Your healing work. Grant me Your enabling grace to complete any and all tasks You desire of me. After having done all to stand, help me stand. Open my heart to grasp the great love of Your heart that motivates everything You ask of me. In the name of Jesus, the Obedient One, Your Son and our Lord. Amen.

Having Done All: Making it Personal

A. Paul instructs us to "be strong in the Lord and the strength of **His** might." (Eph. 6:10) The things Abba asks **us** to do (Eph. 6:13) flow from His enabling grace that works in us. We are not asked or expected to fight the battle in our own strength. We have been *given* the full armor of God. We simply "take it up." (Eph. 6:13)

In the first three chapters of Ephesians, Paul describes all that Abba has done for us in Christ. He has lavished His love and grace on us (ch. 1). He has delivered us from the enemy's domain and made us alive with Jesus, seating us with Him in the heavens (ch. 2). He loves us more profoundly than we can comprehend and does more for us than we can even ask or think (ch. 3). Abba has done all that and more for us when He adopted us in love (1:4,5).

The last three chapters of Ephesians describe our response to Abba as His new creations and the recipients of His love. Our response involves protecting our spiritual bodies with Abba's spiritual armor (Eph. 6:10-17)). For example, we guard and protect our minds by putting on the helmet of salvation. (We filter everything that desires entrance into our minds and only allow those things that are in keeping with wholeness and life (see also Eph. 4:23). We now "wear" truth and righteousness, the livery of Abba's family (see also Eph. 4:24, 25). Our feet are protected by the Gospel of peace as we walk in love with our spouse; our children, our parents, and one another (see Eph. 5:1 ff). There is power and protection in a unified and loving family and a body of believers.

- Read and meditate on the first three chapters of Ephesians, personalizing all Abba has done for His people. For example in chapter one, verse three, you can say "Blessed be the God and Father of our Lord Jesus Christ, who has blessed **me** with every spiritual blessing in the heavenly places in Christ." Give Abba thanks for each and every blessing as you come to them.

- Read through the description of Abba's armor in Eph. 6:10-17. Meditate upon each component. Ask Abba to show you if you are utilizing every part of His armor or where you are vulnerable to attack. In prayer, listen for His instruction on any course of action He wants you to take to protect or strengthen your spirit-man.

- Although we Christians tend to place less importance on our physical bodies than our spiritual bodies, both are important to Abba. Just as there is a spiritual dimension to wholeness, so also there is a physical dimension to wholeness. As a result, there may be things He wants us to **do** as good stewards of our physical bodies to aid in the process of making us whole. For the most part, common sense will instruct our actions. If we are overweight, a balanced diet and regular exercise normally solve the problem. If we use or abuse harmful substances, then freedom from their control is His desire for us. Ask Abba how He wants you to cooperate with the healing process. If you are not capable of making the necessary changes, ask Him to whom you can go for assistance. Don't be afraid to ask for help! Abba will lead you to prayer partners to help you battle in the power of His Spirit. He may also lead you to health professionals when necessary.

My Thoughts and Prayers

Chapter 8: Travail

"I was mute and silent, I refrained even from good, and my sorrow grew worse. My heart was hot within me, while I was musing the fire burned; then I spoke with my tongue." (Psalm 39:2, 3)

"For nothing is hidden, except to be revealed; nor has anything been secret, but that it would come to light." (Mark 4:22)

"When I kept silent about my sin, my body wasted away through my groaning all day long. . . .I acknowledged my sin to You. . . and said, 'I will confess my transgressions to the Lord'; and You forgave the guilt of my sin." (Psalm 32:3, 5)

"We all carry deep within ourselves a reservoir of tears. It takes only the right key at the right time to unlock them . . . . in God's perfect time, when those tears are released, they can form a vast healing flood."[14] Michael Card

We hide many things in our hearts. Like Mary, the mother of Jesus, we may "treasure" words or memories in our hearts (Luke 2:19) and benefit by such hidden treasures. I officiated at the wedding ceremony of our son, Elijah, and his wife, Brandi. I will always remember the joy and privilege of hearing their vows repeated after me; joining their hands together; blessing them in the name of the Father, Son, and Holy Spirit; and pronouncing them to be husband and wife. I will cherish those memories all my days. I will always treasure the memory of our middle daughter, Erin, returning home from her semester of study in Mexico. Back then you could wait at the gate for arrivals. We hadn't seen her for months. We were on tip toes, so eager to catch a glimpse of her emerging from the tunnel. Then we saw her. We embraced her. And we all wept. What blessed memories to treasure in our hearts!

Unfortunately, we sometimes hide things in our hearts which

do us harm, not good. Those things need to be removed, not stored. We must "let them out" or maybe it would be more accurate to say we need to "get them out!" Abba showed me that the journey to wholeness required the cleansing of my heart from sin and the release from my heart of pain caused by emotional wounds I had suffered. As mentioned in an earlier chapter, I surrendered my past and present sins to Abba during "silent week" (and many times since then!) By confessing and surrendering our sins we are assured of Abba's forgiveness through the blood of Christ Jesus. (1 John 1:9) But I found that Abba also had additional means by which to heal the wounds of my heart.

At the outset of my *Katrina*, I hid my wounds in my heart until they made me sick. I needed to talk to someone! A covered wound festers. It must be opened up to let the poison out. Abba brought people across my path to which I could "spill my guts!" Not just anyone or everyone qualified. Abba sent hand-picked people whom I could trust to maintain a confidence, who had experience dealing with wounded hearts, and who loved me. They were Abba's provision for me to help me take another step out of the pit. By speaking out words that honestly conveyed the bottled-up hurts of my heart, the wounds began to heal.

I also wrote in a prayer journal. Normally, I wrote about my wounds in prayer to Abba before I shared them with other people. During silent week I found I could trust Him with anything and everything in my life. When we pray to Abba, we are in a **safe place**! First, I made my sins, weaknesses, brokenness and fears known to Him, and received His forgiving and healing response (never His rejection). Then, I did not shrink from telling others about hidden things in my heart that needed to be spoken. Knowing I am Abba's beloved child sets me free from the fear of others' opinions of me. Abba used both my written prayers and my words spoken to others to bring healing to my heart.

I wept much. Tears are a catharsis for our souls! Sometimes I wept without identifying any specific hurt or wound in my heart. I just cried because I felt so discouraged, so anxious, so overcome by my circumstances. I cried out to Abba for help, strength and mercy in my trouble.

On a few occasions I did not just weep, I lamented. My laments felt and sounded more like wailing than crying. They released deep and specific grief in my heart. I consider those laments as a gift from Abba. I mentioned earlier that I wrote a letter to my deceased father during my "silent week." As I wrote that letter, I lamented. I grieved over the wasted years and our lost relationship, the relationship I never had with my dad. Here is a portion of my letter to my dad:

Dear Dad,

I'm writing this letter out on paper, even though I know I cannot send it to you as you are in heaven. I guess it is more for my benefit than yours, although I hope you can read it from your "vantage point." Or, perhaps our Father in heaven can convey the message to you. This is so hard for me to write. I want to say things now that I should have said to you while you were alive on earth . . . . I see that ours was a "lost relationship." I am so sorry that I knew so little about you, that I was not a more loving son, and that you died before I became a Christian. I'm sorry that you did not meet my wife, Anita, and that you did not get to know our children . . . . I want you to know that I miss you and wish you were here to make up for the lost years of love and friendship that we never did share. I certainly do hope to see you again someday and then we will have eternity to make up for the lost years!

My grief regarding my dad had been buried in my heart for decades. Little did I realize how Abba, in His great wisdom and mercy, would use my *Katrina* to heal so many seemingly unrelated deep wounds in my heart!

At the right time, Abba helped me lament specifically over my *Katrina*. One of the books Melba (the chaplain and counselor mentioned earlier) lent me was *A Sacred Sorrow* by Michael Card. One portion of his book examines the life and laments of King David. At the end of that section he instructs the reader to read through a number of David's Psalms of lament, one of them being Psalm 55. After reading the assigned Psalms, he asks the reader to spend quiet time with the Lord, not seeking to understand the laments but to "enter into" them; allowing David's sorrow, frustration, etc. to mingle with our own.[15] I followed Michael Card's instructions. I read through each of the Psalms he mentioned without emotion. Thinking I had no more "laments" in me. I then prayed a simple prayer asking Abba to help me enter into any lament that He deemed applicable. Immediately, the words of Psalm 55 resounded in my mind and out of my soul burst a torrent of weeping; a lament of grief I had not yet released.

"For it is not an enemy who reproaches me, then I could bear it. . . . But it is you . . . . my companion and my familiar friend . . . . His speech was smoother than butter, but his heart was war; His words were softer than oil, yet they were drawn swords." (Psalm 55: 12, 13, 21) The terrible truth of those words for David and the wound he sustained pierced my heart with a similar agony. As I lamented, I uttered two sentences: "He was my brother, but he stabbed me!" and "He stole my joy!" Amazingly, as suddenly as the lament began it also abruptly ended after several minutes. Only

Abba knows what that lament accomplished, but I know that in His goodness He accomplished something good.

Beloved child of Abba, what hides in your heart? Sins? Resentment? Wounds? Bitterness? Pain? Hurt? If we keep them hidden we are only hurting ourselves. Let them out! Get them out! Open your heart first to Abba. He is **safe**! Then allow Him to help you release the poison inside you. He will lead you to someone you can trust so you can talk about those things hidden in your heart. If necessary and appropriate, He will help you lament. Deep grief requires more than tears, it requires laments. Abba wants to help you! He understands your wounds. He is well acquainted with grief (Isaiah 53:3). He has first-hand experience in lamenting (Lamentations 2:11-13; Mt. 23:37-39). He has the means and the desire to bring you to wholeness. Trust His heart!

Prayer: Abba, search my heart. Show me anything dwelling within that needs to be uprooted and removed. I ask You to cleanse my heart from defilement and mend the hidden wounds. To my extracted sins, add the antidote of the Savior's blood. To my hidden but now unearthed wounds apply Your healing balm. Thank You dear Abba that You are touched by my griefs. Thank You for Your tender love that flows from Your tender heart! Amen.

Travail: Making it Personal

What memories hide within your heart? If you are like most people, there are memories both joyful and grievous hidden inside. When joyful memories emerge, we can give thanks to Abba for blessing our lives with good things. Every time my wife and I walk past the outdoor garden where our youngest daughter was married, we stop and give Abba thanks for her life, for the husband He provided for her, and for other memories of that day. When painful memories emerge, we need not bury them. Abba frequently stirs up a painful memory and brings it to our conscious mind so that He can generate healing deep within us.

As I meditated upon my Katrina, I drew a diagram of the room where I was wounded. There were nine people present including me. I labeled the place where each person sat. Jesus said that He would never leave us nor forsake us. I wanted to know where He was during that devastating experience. I allowed Jesus to bring the memory of that room and the encounter back to my consciousness. I asked Him where He was. At the time of my Katrina, I didn't think He was present at all, but now, months later, as I prayerfully replayed the scene in my heart and mind, I saw that Jesus was in fact in the room through the whole ordeal. Where was He? He was standing behind me with His hands on my shoulders. I suddenly remembered the thoughts that came to me when the verbal blows fell: "Relax! Breathe! I'm here!"

For the following exercise, you may want to be with an experienced prayer partner.

- Ask the Holy Spirit to lead you (He will always lead you gently) to a part of your past that He wants to heal. If a painful memory comes forth, ask Jesus to accompany you back in time to the scene and setting where you were wounded or hurt. Ask Jesus to let you hear and see what He desires for you to hear and see. Jesus is not trying to hurt you but heal you, by exposing the wound to His love, His light, and His presence. He wants to remove the poison from the wound. As you relive the scene, ask Jesus to reveal to you where He was and what He was doing and saying when you received your wound. It may be helpful to sketch a picture or diagram of the location where your wound was received.

- Ask Jesus to help you forgive the person or persons who hurt you. Ask Him to help you pray for them and love them.

My Thoughts and My Prayers

Chapter 9: Come Unto Me

"Come to Me, all you who are weary and heavy-laden, and I will give you rest. Take My yoke upon you and learn from me, for I am gentle and humble in heart, and you will find rest for your souls. For My yoke is easy and My burden is light." (Matthew 11:28-30)

"I have manifested Your name to the men whom You gave Me. . .; they were Yours and You gave them to Me. . . ." (John 17:6)

"He who has the Son has the life; he who does not have the Son of God does not have the life."
(1 John 5:12)

Somewhere on my journey out of the pit I noticed several transitions. For months, Jesus had been leading me to Abba. In Matthew 11:27, Jesus states: ". . . and no one knows the Son except the Father; nor does anyone know the Father except the Son, and anyone to whom the Son wills to reveal Him." Sometimes holding my hand and other times carrying me, Jesus brought me to the heart of Abba. I saw in His heart a deep love for me, deeper than any I had ever known. As Jesus intends, I am discovering that I am also Abba's beloved son. My heart overflows with gratitude to Jesus for revealing His Abba to me, but that was not the end of my journey. I came to Abba and found that He loves me. He wants to spend time with me, and wants what is best for me. He also wants me to follow His Son, Jesus. After being brought to Abba by Jesus, Abba then pointed me back to His Son. The Life Abba wants for us is found in His Son. (1 John 1:1,2; 5:11,12)

In the Scripture quoted above (Mt. 11:27), Jesus says that no one knows the Son except the Father. How then can we get to know the Son? In the next verse (Mt.11:28) Jesus gives us the answer: "Come unto me!" Like Abba, Jesus also welcomes us with open arms. Into those arms Abba directed me. Jesus invites us to come to Him and learn from Him. He wants to exchange His yoke which He calls easy or pleasant, not a heavy burden, for our current yokes which are often characterized as burdensome and worrisome.

When the Bible speaks of yokes, it generally refers to types of masters. Pharaoh's yoke upon the children of Israel was harsh and cruel. Their yoke of affliction directly reflected the character of their master. Forced to meet impossible quotas, they were verbally and physically abused and demoralized. They groaned under the heavy burden of Pharaoh's yoke (Ex.5 and 6 for example). Through prior conditioning and experiences with human authority, many of us expect Jesus' (and God's) yoke to resemble the harsh yoke of servitude imposed by Pharaoh. But with revolutionary and transforming love, Jesus offers us His yoke which is nothing like our fearful expectations. I can scarcely imagine a yoke that is pleasant and a burden that is not burdensome. Yet, our gentle Master promises us that His yoke produces blessed rest, the cure for our burdened and anxiety-filled lives.

In Luke 10:38-42, the sisters, Mary and Martha, offer a vivid contrast of expectations and notions about Jesus. Martha believed that her harried service was exactly what Jesus expected of her, the yoke He required her to bear. She assumed Jesus would join her in denouncing the inactivity of Mary. Mary, on the other hand, sat at Jesus' feet *listening* to Him, learning from Him by attending to His words. She came to Jesus and found peace and rest in His presence. That place and position of peace is precisely what Jesus desired for Martha also. Instead, she was worried and bothered about so many things; no rest, no peace, only demands and burdens. The very kind of yoke one would expect from a Pharaoh god. Mary understood the heart of Jesus and chose the good part, the one necessary thing: "Come unto Me and learn from Me and you shall find rest for your souls."

In the pleasant yoke of Jesus, we learn peace and rest. We also learn humility. Jesus is meek and humble of heart. Like the twelve apostles, the desire for greatness commonly plagues Jesus' present-day followers. As a pastor of a small church, I was ever discontent. I thought I deserved a larger, more exalted position. I envied others whom I deemed less worthy, yet who seemed more successful. As Jesus noted, the proud Pharisees tend to see themselves favorably and look on others with contempt (Luke 18:9). I preached against the pharisaical attitudes of many Christians only to discover I was a closet Pharisee. Jesus revealed to me that those I dismiss as unimportant or unworthy are valuable to Him. My contempt or lack of concern was contrary to His heart. He now prompts me to pray for people, not judge them or ignore them as though they don't exist. He died for them as He did for me. Like the self-righteous elder brother from the parable of the Prodigal Son (Luke 15), I wanted to approach Abba as though I were superior to my brother. But I'm also a sinner and in need of mercy. It is the Prodigal who, humbling himself (". . . make me as one of your hired men. . ." 15:19), receives the hugs, the kisses and the joyous celebration. Slowly but surely, Jesus is teaching me humility.

Being the best and therefore highly esteemed, having preeminence, and desiring the top position, are only a few manifestations of pride. They are the opposite of humility. Jesus invites us to be free from that wearisome life of self-exaltation and ambition. What a burden to always have to be the best; to prove ourselves over and over again; never to relax our guard lest someone get ahead of us (or stay ahead of us); always worried that another person may spot a weakness or an imperfection in us, thus lowering our reputation and disqualifying us as *the greatest*. Jesus has a better idea. Instead of the desire for greatness driven by pride, Jesus suggests we learn from Him humility–lowering ourselves. If we make ourselves last, we never need worry about someone wanting to displace us and we are free from the need to displace others. We need not lose sleep over someone finding an imperfection in us; we have already confessed our weaknesses. There is no need to prove our worth to others so as to maintain our claim of superiority and greatness. We have already abdicated that claim. We have nothing to prove. We don't have to "perform." We need not worry about how others perceive us. Carefully (full of care) protecting our reputation of greatness is unnecessary if we have died to the desire to gain a reputation of greatness. What rest in lowliness! What freedom in humility!

From Jesus we also learn to love. How Jesus loved! He loved (and still loves) children, lepers, prostitutes, His disciples, the crowds, and of course His Father. He loved the least and the last. He had compassion on the needy. He healed broken hearts and broken bodies. He gave His life for us so we could be reconciled to Abba. He did all this because He loved. If we come to Jesus, He will teach us how to love. The lessons will not be directed primarily to the learning center of our heads, but to our hearts. As Jesus drew me closer to Himself, He started a process of filling my heart with His love. This work inside of me is a joint project, a collaboration between Abba, His Spirit and Jesus. I claim absolutely no credit for the work being done. I am more a hindrance to the process than a help. I marvel at Jesus' loving patience with me and His gentle persistence.

I noticed another transition--my tears. As Abba was bringing me out of the pit, my tears flowed readily as a result of my hurt, pain, discouragement, and self-pity. Those tears did not disappear immediately, but I began to weep for other reasons besides those just mentioned. I began to weep in longing for Jesus. I wept because I desired a more intimate relationship with Him. I wept because I wanted to come to Him and learn from Him and walk with Him. When Abba directed me to Jesus, He also put a longing in my heart to seek Jesus. Sometimes the longing is manifested in tears. Another change in my tears became manifest in prayer. Weeping in prayer was not totally foreign to me, but it was the rare exception, not the rule. As Jesus began teaching my heart, I noticed that I wept regularly when interceding for others. In a small measure, He helped me tune in to His heart's frequency of love and compassion as I prayed for others.

Abba sent me to Jesus so I could learn from Him. Actually, Abba did not just send me to Jesus, He *gave* me to Jesus (John 17:6). Just as a human father gives his child to be married to her groom, Abba gave me into the arms of Jesus, the "Lover of my soul," the heavenly bridegroom. Giving me to His Son did not reflect a diminished love for me; it reflected Abba's desire that I live an abundant life of blessed wholeness. That life can only be found in Jesus. By losing our lives, we find real life in Him. This is not a change to dread but to whole-heartedly welcome! Jesus offers to exchange our life which is full of struggle and toil, like a heavy burden, for His Life which is likened to an easy or pleasant task where the burden becomes a pleasure. Jesus assures us that we have nothing to fear in His invitation. He Himself, His very nature, is the guarantee of the life He offers us. He is gentle, pleasant and non-oppressive, just like the life He wants to give us.

I recently gave our youngest daughter, Gwendolyn, to be married to Aaron, the fine young man we had been praying for throughout her and his life (not knowing who he was specifically). I can assure you that my love for my daughter was not in the least bit diminished in my giving her away! On the contrary, I think I loved her more than ever! When I saw Abba was giving me to His Son, the heavenly Bridegroom, I asked my daughter what it was like to be given to her husband. What thoughts or emotions accompanied the experience? This was her response:

> How did it feel to be given to your husband/groom by
> your father? "Well, the excitement and anticipation
> of being with the groom is so great that I had to
> intentionally savor and focus on each interaction with
> you so that I could pay the honor, respect and love
> that was due you. . . .What emotions? Again, the
> emotions were mainly directed towards Aaron and
> the covenant that was about to take place with him.
> The emotions I had toward you were present as you
> spoke and as you gave your exhortation and blessing.

But . . . I knew that I was there for another purpose that day -- to rejoice and celebrate the one for whom God created me, Aaron."

Beloved children of Abba, we are part of the bride of Christ! We are a gift from Abba to Jesus, the "Lover of our souls." We are to be yoked with Him. How should we feel about such a relationship with the King of glory? I suggest my daughter's response would be perfectly fitting: anticipating our coming to Jesus with great excitement! To rejoice and celebrate the One for whom Abba has created us! Oh how Jesus loves us. He invites us to find in Him all we ever hoped for and longed for. He invites us to come to Him. Let's run to Him with joyous anticipation!

Prayer: Dear Abba, thank You for creating me for Your Son, the Lord of heaven and earth and the Lord of life here and now. O Jesus, thank you for inviting me to come unto You! You promised those who seek will would find. By Your grace I come now seeking You and the life found only in You. I eagerly anticipate the joy and peace of being yoked with You. I rejoice in the life shared with You. Teach me I pray, Jesus!   Amen.

Come Unto Me: Making it Personal

Love is a joint project. We are loved by both Abba and Jesus. 1 John 1:3 tells us that our fellowship is with the Father and His Son, Jesus Christ. We are part of a love triangle!

- Picture the Father and the Son standing side-by-side. They are in perfect harmony with arms around each other's shoulders. They are fellowshipping with one another and loving one another through the medium of the Spirit. Now picture yourself invited by both the Father and the Son to stand between them so that their intimate love and fellowship now includes you! They gladly welcome you into their embrace and communion. Love is flowing to you and through you from both Abba and Jesus. Ask the Spirit to make that truth a transforming reality in your life. Listen for them to speak to your heart.

Jesus invites us to come to Him to find life–True Life! It is the life we were created for, Jesus' abundant life manifested in our true selves. I recently had a dream. I saw a cow standing. The cow looked normal except that it had no face. I could see the outline of its head, but there was no face. I saw that cow off-and-on all through the night. Every time I saw it, I heard the words, "till we have faces." Even in my dream I recognized those words as the title of a C.S. Lewis (1956) book which I had never read. The next day, I checked the book out of the library and read it; the message of the book profoundly affected me. I had to lose my old self (represented by a face covered by a veil in the book), in order to find my true life in Christ (my true face uncovered). Abba's ultimate and loving purpose for my Katrina is for me to find and live the "life that is Christ." That is His ultimate purpose for you also.

- Ask Jesus to teach you what it means to put on His yoke and rest in Him.

- Pray for a hunger to find the life for which Jesus created you; the life He wants to live in and through you.
- If you feel so inspired, prayerfully read the book, *Till We Have Faces* (C.S. Lewis)[16]. Please note that the redeeming message in this book is far more subtle than in other Lewis writings.

My Thoughts and My Prayers

Chapter 10: Others

"A new commandment I give to you, that you love one another, even as I have loved you. . . ." John 13:34

"We love, because He first loved us." 1 John 4:19

"Little children let us not love with word or with tongue, but in deed and truth." 1 John 3:18

"Transformation and intimacy both cry out for ministry. We are led through the furnace of God's purity not just for our own sake but also for the sake of others. We are drawn up into the bosom of God's love not merely to experience acceptance but also so we can give his love to others." [17] Richard Foster

Years ago, General Booth of the Salvation Army was scheduled to address the national convention of the Salvation Army in Indianapolis. He became ill and was not able to attend but sent a message to be read instead. During the plenary service, an official came to the podium with envelope in hand to read General Booth's message to the commissioners. He opened the envelope. The message consisted of one word--**OTHERS.**

John tells us that if God abides in us, and we are born of Him, then, in response to His love, we will also love one another. (1 John 4:7-10)

Both Abba and Jesus want us to know the vast and immeasurable love they have for us. Perhaps beyond comprehension, they have the same love for us that they have for one another! (John 17:24) They want to transform us by their love. That transformation will impact others. As Jesus teaches us and fills us with His love, we are weaned from a self-centered existence. We learn to love as He loves. We soon discover that the love of Jesus focuses on others, not ourselves. As mentioned in the previous chapter, intercession is one manifestation of loving others. But Jesus will likely lead us to love, not only in words and prayers but also in deeds.

As she prayed for me one night, my wife "saw" with her heart that the hand of Abba was writing upon my heart. I started praying for Abba to inscribe on my heart and in my life those things He wants written there. One clear message He continues to write upon my heart is to love others. Paul uses the same imagery in 2 Corinthians, chapter 3. He tells that body of believers that he needs no letters of commendation to or from them because **they** are the letter of commendation written upon Paul's heart. In other words, Paul does not need any confirmation from others to vouch for his sincere love and concern for the church at Corinth. Anyone with eyes to see can discern the love which the Spirit of God has written upon Paul's heart for that church. My heart increasingly receives the beautiful etchings of love from Abba's tender hand.

I felt I should read Malachi and Ephesians during this step out of the pit. At least one parallel I saw in these two books was the emphasis God places on relationships. Both books begin with our relationship to Abba; He loves us and wants us to love Him in return. Then in both books, Abba reveals the burden of His heart that brothers and sisters, husbands and wives, parents and children should all be reconciled and relate to each other in love. Early on in my journey to wholeness, Abba began rekindling within me a love for my wife and children. I remember reading the story of Noah during my "Silent Week." I saw that after he awakened from his drunken stupor, Noah unreasonably cursed his son and grandson. His angry words had a lasting and devastating impact! Abba used that Scripture to reveal the destructive effect my anger has had on those closest to me. I have not ceased thanking Him for restoring my relationships with my family.

Abba proceeded to knit my heart together with members of

my extended family with whom I had not been close. Some of my relatives not only thought I did not love them, but that I didn't even like them! In part, my hard heart was to blame, but I also feared the vulnerability and self-exposure of loving others. But Jesus opened His heart to the whole world, knowing He would be rejected and killed by those whom He came to save. The love relationship He had with His Abba sustained Him through it all. We need fear no rejection when we know Abba's loving acceptance.

Abba and Jesus have also deepened my love for others with whom I used to share only a distant friendship. At times Abba has even given me a love for total strangers that I could not have produced myself. My wife and I attended a Christian conference. I was asked to serve the bread of the Eucharist during the final meeting of the conference. As I placed the wafer in the cupped hands of the recipients, I would say, "The body of Christ, broken for you." One gentleman had on his name tag. As I said the words, "Franklin, the body of Christ broken for you," I was overcome with Jesus' love for this man. I wept and he wept as we touched foreheads together. Abba's Spirit wrote Franklin's name in my heart, though we'd never met.

As I meditated in the book of Malachi, I saw that throughout my journey to wholeness, Abba had been restoring the very relationships mentioned in that book. He brought me to intimacy with Himself; He rekindled my love for my wife and my children; He restored my broken relationships with brothers and sisters in Christ. Abba revealed His well-ordered plan from Malachi in order to confirm and cement the gracious work He had been doing in my heart. But more than that, He was inviting me to participate in His heart's desire, the work of reconciling people to Him and others.

Jesus wants to love the lost, the lonely, and the broken through us whether they are family members or not. The theme of Luke's Gospel plainly reveals the heart of Jesus, and therefore the heart of Abba. "For the Son of Man came to seek and save that which is lost." (Luke 19:10) In Hannah Hurnard's book, *Hinds' Feet on High Places*, the young lady, *Much-Afraid*, is led on a journey to wholeness by the Good Shepherd. Through the process, the Good Shepherd transforms her and gives her a new name, *Grace and Glory*. Now upon the heights of the Shepherd King's kingdom, she and her King gaze down upon the valley she called home and from whence she began her journey. Grace and Glory suddenly perceives the purpose for which her King brought her to that vista.

> Suddenly she understood. She was beholding a wondrous and glorious truth; (He desired) a great multitude. . . brought like herself by the King to the Kingdom of Love . . .so they could pour out their lives is gladdest abandonment, leaping down with him to the sorrowful, desolate places below, to share with others the life which they had received. She herself was (to be) only one drop among that glad, exultant throng of Self-givers, the followers of the King of Love, united with him and with one another, each one equally blessed and beloved as herself.[18]

Jesus teaches us to follow Him as He reaches out to *others*, not motivated by guilt, manipulation, pride or even duty, but as a labor of love. Paul addresses these words to the Corinthians: "For the *love of Christ* (my emphasis) controls us. . . . that they who live might no longer live for themselves, but for Him who died and rose again on their behalf." (2 Cor. 5:14) Jesus brought me to Abba and I learned how much Abba loves me. Abba gave me back to Jesus and I am learning how much Jesus loves people, especially hurting people; that includes almost everybody.

Prayer: Dear Abba, in love You sought me. In love You restore and transform me. In love You gave me to Your Son, Jesus. Now, Jesus, teach me to reach out to the hurting in Your Name and with Your love. May the results be nothing short of glorious! Thank You, Abba! Thank You, Jesus!

Others: Making It Personal

My wife and I have been amazed as we witness Jesus setting up "divine appointments" for us with other people. Sometimes those appointments are with people we know, but often they are not. Sometimes we know about the appointment in advance, but frequently we do not discover Jesus' intended purpose until the encounter takes place. The following is one such example.

I recently went to help a family unload a moving van on the other side of the county, about 45 minutes from home. When I arrived I found they had completed the task. My first reaction was to regret the waste of my time. But on my return home, I wondered if there might be some other reason I would be in this part of the county, a purpose I did not yet understand. Driving near the downtown area of our county seat, I had a sudden impulse to exit on a street which leads to the center of town. This part of the city is very diverse, both the stores and the clientele. On a number of occasions, I had made forays into the city to sow seeds of Abba's love, mostly with shop-workers. I had already developed some friendships with several such folk.

After parking, I made several visits to people I had previously met. They were "positive" encounters, yet I wasn't convinced I had yet found the reason for my trip. I was walking back to the car and at a corner just half a block from the car, when a young woman approached the same corner from a side street. Our paths converged at that corner. In the few seconds it took to pass her, I received several impressions: She was not from this area, she was younger than my daughters, she had not bathed in quite a while, and everything she owned was in her backpack. What I saw clearly was a young woman with nose and lip rings, walking barefoot with her boots hanging over her shoulder. As I passed her I said, "You are barefoot." (Brilliant insight!) "It's hot," was her reply. I took two more steps toward my car before my forward progress was arrested by Jesus. I stopped and did an about face and began what turned into a five hour conversation and encounter with 19 year old Polly (not her real name). We walked and talked. We drank coffee and tea and talked. All the while I prayed silently: "Jesus, how can I help this girl? How do You want me to love her?" I felt certain that Polly was my reason for coming to the city, but I didn't know why. I found several opportunities to pray aloud. Polly was sick so I prayed out loud for Jesus to heal her. She "tolerated" my prayers but did not try to encourage them.

I slowly pieced together some of her story. Polly had just arrived a few days earlier from Chicago. She came to this area with the hopes of getting a job on a farm where a friend of hers works. She was wandering the rainy streets with a bad cough and cold, waiting for the friend to call her cell phone and arrange a ride to lodging for the night. She was supposed to have an interview with the owner of the farm the next day. Out of curiosity, I asked if she knew the name of the owner of the farm. She knew the first name– "Annie." My heart skipped a beat. I know a family who owns a farm. He is the doctor who delivered our daughters. Both he and his wife are dear friends of ours. Their daughter uses their farm to raise and sell organic vegetables; the daughter's name? **Annie**. With trembling voice I asked Polly if she knew Annie's husband's name. "Isaiah." she replied. My mouth dropped open. I could hardly believe it! I had been wandering the streets of the city with this lost lamb, praying how best to help her and love her, only to find out that she hoped to get a job at a farm owned by our friends. When I told her the connection I have to that family, her mouth dropped open. She said: "That's an amazing coincidence!" Trying to contain my excitement, I responded: "No, Polly, it is not a coincidence. It is Jesus saying, 'I love you Polly!' as clearly as if He had written it in the sky!" Her lip trembled, but having been wounded so deeply, she steeled herself against any emotion-laughter *or* tears. I called my friend, Annie's father, and told him the short version of the story. With his approval, I drove Polly to the farm myself instead of waiting for her friend to call her. I introduced Polly to my friends who own the farm. They welcomed us with open arms and fed us both. Polly did have the interview the next day and was given the job. My wife and I are now praying how Jesus wants us (or will allow us) to be part of Polly's life.

The more I contemplate my encounter with Polly, the more amazed I become. There is no doubt in my mind that we were meant to come into contact, that we had kept a divine appointment. Our meeting depended on a five second window of opportunity. Five seconds later or earlier for either of us to arrive at that corner and we would never have met. The only difference between this encounter and the disciples' encounter with the man carrying the water jar (Luke 22:10), is that those disciples were told specifically who to look for in advance. Jesus arranged the meeting between Polly and I because of His great love for a 19 year lost lamb that He wanted found.

- Jesus wants to use you to reach out to others who are lost or wounded or both. It is an awesome privilege and a joy to be a part of His ministry! As you spend time in fellowship with Jesus, ask Him to fill you with His love for others. Pray that He would open your eyes to see the "divine appointments" He brings across your path. Listen for any directions He may want to give you. If you do not see immediate results, don't get discouraged! Continue to open your heart to Jesus, absorbing His love for you and offering your life to Him. He **will** send you to others, or send others to you- probably both!

My Thoughts and My Prayers

Chapter 11: Wait and Hope

"I waited patiently for the Lord; and he inclined to me and heard my cry." (Psalm 40:1)

"I would have despaired unless I had believed that I would see the goodness of the Lord in the land of the living. Wait for the Lord; be strong and let your heart take courage; yes, wait for the Lord." (Psalm 27:13, 14)

"So there remains a Sabbath rest for the people of God. For the one who has entered His rest has himself also rested from his works, as God did from His." (Hebrews 4:9, 10)

"Commit your way to the Lord, trust also in Him and He will bring it to pass." (Psalm 37:5) "The way will open, the right issue will come, the end will be peace, the cloud will be lifted, and the light of eternal noonday shall shine at last." (Commentary from *Streams in the Desert* by Mrs. Charles Cowman on Psalm 37:5)[19]

If you choose to skip over this chapter, I wouldn't blame you one bit! I often feel that I would like to skip over it also–waiting, that is. Several years ago our daughter, Erin, having graduated from college, felt that God would have her **wait** on Him for the next step in her life. As the weeks of waiting turned into months, I put increasing pressure on her at least to look for part-time work while she waited for God to reveal a bigger plan. She remained adamant in her belief that she **was** following God's plan. Admittedly, she was not sitting around and watching TV or wasting her time with other "couch potato" activities. She read and studied and prayed and wrote. Eventually, in Abba's perfect time, He opened the perfect door for our daughter and other doors since then. I wouldn't be surprised if the irony of the situation gives you a good chuckle. Here I am, having doubted the path my daughter took, now following in her steps! I am not *just* waiting either, but reading many of the same books, studying some of the same subjects, and writing, just like my daughter did. I am learning that sometimes waiting is part of Abba's plan. Therefore, there must be something good and important to receive from Him in the process though we long for our release. Abba does not waste time. He does all things for a reason and the end results will be good.

Waiting is a biblical idea with numerous examples. Moses waited forty years in the wilderness, tending sheep and raising a family. Then, finally (and unexpectedly) Yahweh called him and revealed His mission to him. Only Abba sees when all circumstances are right for the next step; when all the people and conditions are perfectly aligned for His plan to be unveiled and His purposes fulfilled. Among other lessons, Moses undoubtedly learned much about shepherding people from his experience of shepherding sheep. In addition, there was a perfect time and a specific cast of characters necessary before the Exodus could take place upon the world's stage. We do not understand many of Abba's reasons for waiting, but we can trust that He knows what is best and that He does all things well.

When people ask me what I am doing these days, I respond: "I am waiting and praying." (I often think of my daughter when I answer!) I long for the day when I can offer another response, but for now I cannot. By "waiting" I do not mean "inactivity" either on my part or God's part. During this "timeout" Jesus is teaching and I am learning. Some months ago, I felt that I should be reviewing and increasing my knowledge of biblical languages and Spanish. I'm not sure why, but while I wait I am studying those languages. I hope to discover the reason behind those studies, but even if I don't, I will have gained from the experience.

Jesus continues to teach me to pray, especially to listen with my heart. I want to hear the voice of my Abba with greater clarity and frequency. Being a left-brained "thinker," it is not easy for me to hear with my heart. Through books, through meditation, through experiential training with others, through solitude, and by the help of the Holy Spirit, I am slowly learning to hear Abba's voice with my heart. (I am also learning that Jesus is a very patient and loving teacher.) If learning to hear Abba's voice were the only thing learned or gained by my waiting, the time will have been well spent. I know of nothing that compares with hearing the loving voice of Abba while in intimate communion with Him.

Hudson Taylor's favorite hymn was "Jesus, I Am Resting" by Jean Sophia Piggott. (1876)

Jesus, I am resting, resting,
In the joy of what Thou art;
I am finding out the greatness
Of Thy loving heart.
Thou hast bid me gaze upon Thee,
And Thy beauty fills my soul,
For by Thy transforming power,
Thou hast made me whole.

When difficult situations arose in his life, Hudson Taylor would start humming or singing that hymn to remind himself of Jesus' faithfulness and loving oversight of his life. Taylor's conclusion: We strengthen faith, not by striving after faith, but resting on the Faithful One.[20]

When I understood that Jesus was calling me to come unto Him (chapter 9), I realized that He wanted me to find **rest** in Him. For me, the ability to completely *rest* in Jesus has not transpired overnight. During my time of waiting, Jesus continues to teach me to be at peace within by resting in Him. He is also showing me that *rest* is the fruit of **trust.** As a very practical example, can we **trust** Him to meet all our needs while I am waiting and not working? If we trust Him, then we will rest and have peace; if we do not, then we will become anxious or restless. Jesus is the Master teacher. He teaches us truths not just in theory, He fleshes them out in life-experiences; much the same way as when He fed the five thousand with loaves of bread, then taught them that He is the *bread of life* (John 6); or, when He told His disciples that He is the Light of the World, then He opened the eyes of the man born blind (John 9).

One such life-experience lesson reinforced Jesus' teaching and His desire for us to hear Abba's voice **and** to trust Him with our finances; two lessons rolled up into one experience.
My wife and I thought that Abba wanted us to make a 700 mile trip (one way) to see my mother over Thanksgiving. She lives on a nursing-care floor of a retirement facility. Due to my wife's work schedule, we would have only five days to make the trip and we really could not afford the expense. We prayed and asked Abba to confirm His plan by sending us money to cover the cost of the trip. The day arrived for our departure. We would leave at 2 PM from my wife's workplace. No money had yet arrived and there was no expected source of funds that we were aware of. As my quiet time that morning (a time of fellowship with Abba where I also listen for His voice) came to a close, I simply asked one more time, "Papa, is there anything You would like to say to me before I finish?" I thought I heard an unusual reply: "I'll tell you during your Hebrew lesson." The book I use to study Hebrew has the student translate sentences as part of the learning process. I could only imagine that Abba would speak to me from one or more of those exercises. At the customary hour, I began to work through the day's lesson. I eagerly looked for an "epiphany" but the practice sentences that day seemed very dull and uninspired. I soon decided that I only imagined Abba's message and simply focused on my study. About half way through my study time, the phone rang–it was my wife. Her first words were: "Are you sitting down?" I wasn't but I immediately did, wondering if something were wrong. She proceeded to tell me that she just received a totally unexpected check from her employer. The amount would pay for our trip with enough left over to pay our property taxes which were due in just two weeks (another need we had been praying about). As she relayed this exciting news to me, I suddenly remembered Abba's words spoken to my heart that

morning, the words I had all but discredited. "I'll tell you during your Hebrew lesson." Overwhelmed by His love, I rejoiced with tears.

We did make the trip to see my mom. It was one of the most amazing five days we have ever experienced! We felt as though we were in a great river of Abba's presence and plan. We were being swept along in the current of His love. Every step of the way He surprised us with gifts of grace and guided us by means out of the ordinary. Above all, we learned a bit more of what Jesus was trying to teach us: "Listen with your heart for Abba's voice and trust me!" Those lessons and more are gifts to those who wait.

Prayer: Dear Abba, waiting is so difficult for me! Please encourage my heart. Continue Your work of transformation in my heart and life. I long to spend time with You and hear Your tender voice with the ears of my heart. Jesus, with You as my close companion, help me come to know that though I am alone, I need not be lonely. Help me rest in You. One day soon may I look back on this time of waiting with wonder and thanksgiving, seeing how You have used it for good. Thank You, Abba. Amen.

Wait and Hope: Making It Personal

I recently read *The Count of Monte Cristo* by Alexandre Dumas (1894). The protagonist, Edmond Dantes, is falsely accused, betrayed, and thrown into prison. Initially he despairs of ever being released or escaping from his prison. His confinement is all the more grievous because he sees no one but the jailer. Finally, Edmond meets a priest who tunnels into his cell by accident. Edmond and the priest spend hours together daily. The learned and wise priest begins to teach him many things, including languages, so that after one year "Edmond was a new man." Edmond pays the following tribute to the priest: "My real treasure is your presence, living together five or six hours a day. . . . to hear your eloquent voice that embellishes my mind, strengthens my soul, and makes my whole frame capable of great and terrible things."[21]

- While you are waiting (it may seem like a prison at times), Jesus wants to give you the treasures of experiencing His presence and hearing His voice. Ask Jesus, our High Priest, to help you receive those treasures and be transformed by them. Ask Him what other treasures He wants you to receive.

At the conclusion of the book, Edmond (now the Count) writes a letter to a young couple whom he rescued from a seemingly hopeless situation. Here is his advice: "Love and be happy, beloved children of my heart and never forget, that until the day God will deign to reveal the future to man, all human wisdom is contained in these two words: **wait** and **hope**."[22]

- Pray for Jesus to fill you with patience and expectancy as you *wait* and *hope*.

My Thoughts and My Prayers

Chapter 12: In the Fullness of Time: My Feet Upon A Rock

". . . in the fullness of time, God sent forth His Son. . ." Gal. 4:4

"But as for me, I trust in You, O Lord. I say, 'You are my God. My times are in Your hand.'" Psalm 31:14, 15

". . . in Your book were written all the days that were ordained for me, when as yet there was not one of them. How precious also are Your thoughts to me, O God! How vast is the sum of them!" Psalm139:16,17

"It can't be done. By this I remember that I can't arrange for the life I prize. . . .(this) does not discourage me; quite the contrary, it frees my heart from the grasping and plotting and fretting over my life. . . It reminds me to let it go. It breaks the power of the spell the evil one is trying to weave around us."[23] John Eldredge

"He brought me up out of the pit of destruction, out of the miry clay, and He set my feet upon a rock. . ." Psalm 40:2

I am still no expert at waiting! Like the redeemed of Revelation, I sometimes cry out, "How long O Lord?!" But I also find myself meditating more and more on God's perfect timing and perfect plan. He sent His Son to earth "in the fullness of time." Although we can speculate about the reasons for God's timing in the sending of His Son, only He has the full picture. That is true for our lives also. Abba knows the plans He has for us and those plans include a perfect timing and unfolding "in the fullness of time."

I often contemplate David's trusting words: "My times are in Your hand." (Ps. 31:15). Every time I repeat those words and meditate upon the truth contained in them, I find the same freedom from grasping and fretting of which John Eldredge spoke. My heart is freed from worry over the details of my life; from the moment-by-moment details to the major issues of life.

Stepping out my front door, it seems I have always been in a hurry. I had to reach some destination as soon as possible. I did not want to wait for traffic lights. I was impatient with slow drivers. I had a tendency to speed, or at least get to the next stop light before the car beside me as though I were a contestant in an all-crucial race. These are all symptoms of the belief that "my times are in **my** hands." When my life is in my hands, there is neither peace nor tranquility, just pressure, fretting, and struggling.

Our son and his wife were called to minister at a church in a city over 30 minutes from their home. A move to the new city made sense. They found a subdivision with new construction homes in their price range. After praying, they believed God favored the move. Their new house would be ready in three or four months which meant they had several months to sell their current home. The obligation to purchase their new house was contingent upon the sale of their former home, but the new house would be put on the open market if the former did not sell in time. After the deadline, if no one else purchased the new home, my son and his wife could still buy it, but at a higher price. They quickly spruced up their current home and put it on the market. They waited. They prayed. They waited some more. As the months sped by, they lowered the asking price but still no buyer surfaced. They agonized and we agonized with them. After several months, their new home was ready but their old home had not sold. Greatly discouraged, they let their dream go. Three months after the new home was finished, a contract was signed on their old home. Out of curiosity they checked on the home they had relinquished. It had not yet sold and they were told they could have it for the original price if they could complete all necessary details and transactions in one week, a seemingly impossible task. Amazingly, they moved out of the old and into the new home with only hours to spare. When they had time to reflect about all that had taken place; the delay, the emotional roller coaster and the mystery of God's timing, they discovered they not only obtained the house they had wanted, but due to the lower mortgage payments while still living in their unsold home, they had also saved over one thousand dollars by the delay. Their worries (and ours) were needless and fruitless. God's timing was perfect.

Abba has a perfect and blessed design for our lives. If He cares about the details, He obviously cares about the major decisions and directions for our lives. Yes, I want to know the next step for my life. I want to see His plan unfold. I would like to know what He has been preparing me for. Though I don't know yet, I do know that my times are in His hand, and that while I am waiting, He continues to change me and mold me and transform me until, in the fullness of time, Jesus' likeness is birthed in me.

One month ago, my wife was diagnosed with breast cancer. After other diagnostic tests, one week ago she had a lumpectomy. During the operation, the surgeon took surrounding tissue and lymph nodes for further testing. Today we will see him for her follow-up visit, and also receive the results of her tissue and lymph nodes biopsies. This last month has not been without its anxious moments. But on the other hand, I cannot describe to you the amazing peace Jesus has given us at every turn of our journey. He has been so intimately involved in our lives over the last year; guiding, directing, loving and healing us, that it is inconceivable this major issue in our lives has "slipped by" Him, unnoticed. We **know** that He has a plan. We also know that our times are in His hands and before day one of our lives was lived, they were written down in His book. We know that His thoughts toward us are precious and beyond count.

Many faithful friends and family have been praying for my wife, Anita. We clearly would like all those prayers answered in glorious fashion, resulting in health and wholeness for her and bringing glory to Abba. But regardless of the outcome, and regardless of whether we end up rejoicing or reeling, in this moment of clear thinking and sanity, we know that our times are in Abba's hand and that His thoughts toward us are precious. That is true, regardless.

. . . .nine months later

My wife received her thirty-third and last radiation treatment today. We celebrated! (The margins were not clear but thankfully the lymph nodes were.) I can't explain why my Katrina or my wife's cancer was necessary in Abba's plan for us. I do know, however, that we are more intimately united to Abba and to one another than at any time in our lives. In spite of surgery, chemo, radiation, and all the side effects they have produced, nothing has separated us from the love of Abba and His Son, Jesus. We have been carried by His grace. My wife has hardly missed a day of teaching. Abba has planted my feet more firmly on the rock regardless of the ordeal through which we have just passed.

As my wife has finished up her treatments, doors have been opening up for me. I don't know where these will lead, but we sense the King is on the move and His good plan for our lives is unfolding.

Not long ago, a friend of mine, Jay, related to me the following account.

Jay and his family recently spent three weeks at a cottage on Lake Hartwell. During those three weeks, Jay could only stay at the cottage on the weekends due to his work. While Jay was away, his eleven-year-old son, Caleb, planned a surprise for his dad. On the final weekend, Caleb wanted to be able to swim across the cove from their dock and then back to their dock without a life jacket or other aids, a distance of at least 100 yards each way. So, while Jay was away, Caleb practiced swimming around their dock for increasingly longer periods of time in preparation for the "big day." Finally, on the last weekend, Caleb told his dad about the surprise.

The whole family went down to the dock. Caleb jumped in the water and started for the other side of the cove. Jay swam beside him. Caleb made it to the other side but seemed quite tired. Jay wondered if Caleb would call off the return trip. But upon touching solid ground, Caleb immediately started the return journey. Jay swam beside him as before. About three fourths of the way back, Caleb became tired and obviously began to struggle. At this point Jay had two convictions: 1) He knew that he would not let Caleb go under. 2) It would be really important for Caleb to reach his goal--the ladder of his own dock. Jay fought the strong desire to just sweep Caleb up in his strong arms and tote him to the dock. Happily, Caleb did make it! As soon as Caleb reached the ladder, Jay looked up to see his wife, Laurie, standing on the dock. She had been praying for Caleb the entire journey. Tears streamed down her face. When Caleb climbed the ladder it was to the great and warm embrace of his delighted, weeping mother. Jay told me that story because he believed it paralleled my own story. In the midst of my Katrina, akin to swimming in very deep water, Abba has been swimming by my side. He has not nor would not let me go under! And like Laurie, Jesus has been interceding for me, awaiting me with open arms.

I include this story for the same reason Jay related it to me. In the midst of your circumstances, no matter what they are, Abba is beside you. He will not abandon you nor let you go under. Jesus ever intercedes for you and awaits you with open arms. Do not panic! Do not fear! Trust Abba. His timing is perfect, His grace is sufficient and He loves you!

Prayer: Dear Jesus, assure your hurting children of Your blessed Presence. Come to our aid I pray. Come quickly, please! Deliver us from panic and fear. Gift us with a profound and settled peace that only You can give. Abba, if any one reading this still finds themselves in a pit, I ask that You send them the help they need whether it be from people, literature, or a direct intervention of Your Spirit.

In the Fullness of Time: Making It Personal

Although my wife's radiation treatments normally took no more than one half hour per visit, her first appointment required about two hours to set up and program the machine. She had to raise her arms above her head, placing them in arm supports. She was asked not to move. She wept. She was unable to wipe her tears away because her arms were positioned above her head and she was told not to move them. She could not blink away the tears because her eyelashes fell out during chemo. She felt helpless. At that moment, she remembered Jesus dying on the cross. He couldn't move His arms either. He could not wipe away blood, sweat or tears from His eyes. Jesus understood what Anita was experiencing. Then, she felt Jesus embracing her as she lay helpless on that table.

Jesus knows exactly what you are going through. He dwelt on earth in the flesh in order to identify with us in our sufferings and deliver us from fear. Having been raised from the dead, He now comes to our aid in our sufferings (Hebrews 2:10-18). Pray and ask Jesus to let you experience His warm embrace and His tender love.

Abba, baptize me in Your love.
Jesus, live Your life out in and through me.
Holy Spirit, fill me and empower me to become the person I was created to be and to do the work I was created to do.
Abba, lead me into ever-increasing intimacy with You. Make me whole I pray!

Thank You, Blessed Three!
Amen.

My Thoughts and My Prayers

Epilogue

With a thankful heart I write to relate to you that my wife has recently finished her last Herceptin treatment, has finished the reconstruction process, and has had her port removed (the surgically implanted receptacle for all her chemo and Herceptin treatments). On the eve of her last Herceptin treatment, Anita, unable to sleep, arose at midnight and penned these words:

Faithful and True

Jesus, I thank You that You visit Lions' dens,
Fiery furnaces and Locked prisons.
And in each place, Your Presence makes all the difference:
You shut the mouths of lions,
You are a shield in the midst of flames,
You open prison doors.

Daniel, did Jesus sit by your side
And watch while you slept next to lions?
Meshach, did Jesus walk beside you
As you entered that fiery hell?
Peter, did Jesus stand beside you
As the locked prison door swung wide?

What den, or furnace, or prison are you in today?
Jesus will sit and watch with you,
And shut the lions' mouths.
He will walk with you in the midst of your flames,
And see you come out unscathed.
He will stand with you inside your prison
And swing wide the iron bars with one touch.

Do not despair.
Hope on in prayer.
Rest and trust in the Crucified One.

He alone is Faithful and True,
And He will see you through.

The Lion of Judah is a match to any lion.
The Light of the World can outshine any flame.
The Keeper of the Keys of hell and death can open any prison door.

Do not despair.
Hope on in prayer.
Rest and trust in the Crucified One.
He alone is Faithful and True,
And He will see you through.

Anita Lovejoy

POSTSCRIPT

On Eagles' Wings

For vacation this summer, my wife and I made our yearly pilgrimage to Little Long Lake, one of my favorite places on earth. This natural lake, of modest dimensions, has been a summer destination for my family for nearly 100 years. Some of my fondest boyhood memories stem from the summers spent on this body of water in northern Indiana. My wife and I love to espy the many varieties of birds who call the lake their home. Egrets, kingfishers, loons, and blue herons thrive in this habitat.

Walking down the lane, we met a neighbor who informed us that a new winged inhabitant now dwells at our lake—a golden eagle! I had my doubts about her golden claim, but the very next day I became a believer! Early in the morning, as I sat by the lake, loud splashing arrested my attention. I looked up in time to see a very large dark brown bird hovering over the water about 40 yards from my roost. I witnessed it plunge its talons into the water, and with great, majestic strokes, fly to the top of a tall tree on the other side of the lake with its catch-of-the-day firmly in tow. The beating of the eagle's wings was not hurried or frantic. Each powerful and majestic undulation lifted it higher and higher, overcoming the force of gravity. It was an awesome sight!

As I reflected on what I had seen, I recalled a scene from the book of Exodus. With Moses at their helm, the Children of Israel had just been released by Pharaoh. They followed the prescribed path toward freedom which led them to the edge of the Red Sea. About that time, Pharaoh had yet another change of heart and sent his army to fetch the escaping slaves back to Egypt. Now trapped between the Red Sea and Pharaoh's army, God's people panicked. In the seemingly hopeless situation, they cried out in fear for their lives. But the stalwart Moses calmed them. He told them not to fear, but to trust God. Surely God would save them, Moses attested.

The rest of the story is well known. The Children of Israel walked through the Red Sea on dry ground, but Pharaoh's pursuing army met a watery grave. On the other side of the sea, God spoke to His people with these words (Ex. 19:4): *"You yourselves have seen what I did to the Egyptians and how I bore you on eagles' wings, and brought you to Myself."* In other words, *"Look where you've been and the seemingly hopeless obstacles you faced. Look where you are now. I brought you here on eagles' wings!"* Like the flight of a golden eagle, with great power and majesty, God delivered His people.

I feel the same way! Reflecting back to the beginning of my Katrina through to this present hour, I know that God has brought me to **Himself** as if **on eagle's wings**. This journey with God has forever changed me. Even though my life now looks fairly "normal" on the surface, my heart will never be the same. Not long ago, I confided to a friend that I have never been so broken and yet I have never been so whole. I've never felt Him as close to me as in these last few years. Still, at any given moment and in any location, God might pluck a certain chord in my heart and I am undone. Whether broken or whole or both, I feel like I have been given the greatest of all gifts: **intimacy with Abba's heart.**

Prayer: Majestic Father, wing me to Yourself I pray. Amen.

NOTES

Chapter Two: The Big Picture

[1] Source Unknown; Alan Redpath was born in 1907 and died in 1989. He was a British evangelist, pastor and author. Among the churches he pastored was Moody Church in Chicago.

[2] Dan Allender and Tremper Longman III, *Intimate Allies* (Wheaton, IL: Tyndale House Publishers, 1995)

[3] Ray Simpson, Editor, *Celtic Daily Light: A spiritual journey through the year* (Kevin Mayhew LTD, 2003), January 2 entry.

Chapter Three: The Comfort of Scripture

[4] Richard Foster: *Prayer: Finding the Heart's True Home* (San Francisco: Harper Collins Publishers, 1992), page 144.

Chapter Four: A Blade of Mordor

[5] J.R.R. Tolkein, *The Fellowship of the Ring* (New York: Ballantine Books, 1965).

Chapter Five: Silent Week

[6] Signa Bodishbaugh, *The Journey to Wholeness in Christ* (Grand Rapids: Chosen Books, 1997), page 73.

[7] John Eldredge, *Wild at Heart* (Nashville: Thomas Nelson, Inc., 2001).

[8] Brennan Manning, *Abba's Child* (NavPress, 1994, 2002).

[9] E. Stanley Jones, *A Song of Ascents* (Nashville: Abingdon Press, 1968), page 337.

[10] Henri J.M. Nouwen, *Life of the Beloved* (New York: Crossroad, 1992), page 24.

[11] Richard Foster: *Prayer: Finding the Heart's True Home* (San Francisco: Harper Collins Publishers, 1992).

Chapter Six: How Much More

[12] Hannah Whitall Smith, *The Christian's Secret of a Happy Life* (New York: Fleming H. Revell Co., 1888), page 48.

[13] Bodishbaugh, page 73.

Chapter Eight: Travail

[14] Michael Card, *A Sacred Sorrow* (NavPress, 2005), page 86.
[15] Card, page 92.

Chapter Nine: Come Unto Me

[16] C.S. Lewis, *Till We Have Faces* (PTE Limited, 1956).

Chapter Ten: Others

[17] Foster, page 168.
[18] Hannah Hurnard, *Hinds' Feet on High Places* (Wheaton, IL., Tyndale House, 1988), page 253.

Chapter Eleven: Wait and Hope

[19] Mrs. Charles E. Cowman, *Streams in the Desert* (Los Angeles: Cowman Publications, 1925), page 358.
[20] Dr. and Mrs. Howard Taylor, *Hudson Taylor: God's Man in China* (Chicago: Moody Press, 1971), page 247.
[21] Alexander Dumas, *The Count of Monte Cristo* (New York: Random House, 1996), page 221.
[22] Dumas, page 1462.

Chapter Twelve: In the Fullness of Time: My Feet Upon A Rock

[23] John Eldredge, *The Journey of Desire* (Nashville: Thomas Nelson Publishers, 2000), page 209.